Theodore Hesburgh, C.S.C., presents the findings of four task forces he appointed to examine the relationship of adult and continuing education to social responsibility, public affairs, the role of the college and university, and the rapidly growing body of knowledge. *Paul Miller* analyzes the influence of adult and continuing education on the academic community, the shaping of civic policy, and the creation of new lifestyles. *Clifton Wharton, Jr.,* whose findings are based on the report of a task force he initiated, shows precisely what is required of a large, complex institution to accommodate itself to the education needed by adults in the modern world. *Patterns for Lifelong Learning* describes the strategies of a new philosophy of urgent concern to all those in higher education.

Patterns
for
Lifelong
Learning

A Report of Explorations
Supported by the
W. K. Kellogg Foundation

Theodore M. Hesburgh, C.S.C.
Paul A. Miller
Clifton R. Wharton, Jr.

Patterns
for
Lifelong
Learning

 Jossey-Bass Publishers
San Francisco · Washington · London · 1973

PATTERNS FOR LIFELONG LEARNING
A Report of Explorations Supported by the W. K. Kellogg Foundation
by Theodore M. Hesburgh, C.S.C., Paul A. Miller,
and Clifton R. Wharton, Jr.

Copyright © 1973 by: Jossey-Bass, Inc., Publishers
615 Montgomery Street
San Francisco, California 94111

&

Jossey-Bass Limited
3 Henrietta Street
London WC2E 8LU

Library of Congress Catalogue Card Number LC 73-10936

International Standard Book Number ISBN 0-87589-200-0

Manufactured in the United States of America

JACKET DESIGN BY WILLI BAUM

FIRST EDITION

Code 7349

The Jossey-Bass
Series in Higher Education

CYRIL O. HOULE, *University of Chicago*
Special Advisor, Adult and Continuing Education

Preface

In a nation which already has the world's most elaborate and expensive system of formal education, suggestions for building new systems are likely to fall on deaf ears, especially if they call for greatly increased expenditures of public funds. But most people probably believe that the educational system we have can be improved. In *Patterns for Lifelong Learning* we advocate basic changes in attitudes toward education that can help build new learning systems in tune with the needs of contemporary society. More programs or expenditures may be necessary, but changes in attitudes are equally important.

First, there is a widespread attitude that young people need formal education while adults do not, that the education one receives as a child or young adult is enough to carry one through a lifetime. When knowledge was more stable than now and wisdom was cumulative, there was some reason for highly structured, preestablished curricula for the education of youth. But now much of the knowledge and professional training of a graduate is obsolete fifteen years after graduation unless that education is continually updated through purposeful learning. The worst education is one which produces a person who thinks he or she knows everything, that formal education is finished and left behind. One of the greatest products of a meaningful education is the intellectual curiosity that leads men and women to continued learning and makes them eager to learn as the experience of life reveals areas of ignorance. Whatever is done to improve formal education, nothing is more important than to inculcate students with an understanding that education has to be continuous through life and at the same time to develop their ability to be self-learners.

Second, there is an attitude that education is the same as schooling. As a result, the length of time spent in conventional schooling grows longer. Society has become conditioned to being ever more acquisitive of degrees and credentials, benchmarks of formal schooling, in the vain expectation that more schooling means better education, when often all it signifies is more time spent in school. At some point, there has to be a realization that the aim of all this education is learning and knowledge, not the degrees gained. As this realization grows, it will become even more evident than it is today that much purposeful learning occurs on the job, in the home, and in the business of everyday life; the idea of overextended schooling detracts from the goal of lifelong learning because it assumes that meaningful education is the sole property of educational institutions.

A third attitude, related to the above, is that the business of educators is formal schooling and that they should not be concerned with education that goes on elsewhere. A leader in the airlines industry was once asked how it was that the railroads, which carried so many people across the country in an earlier day, had lost much of this business to buses and airlines. His answer was that the railroads thought they were in the railroad business when they should have realized that they were in the transportation business. We have the same problem in education today. Many people in education on all levels forget they are in education. They think they are in high school education, or postsecondary education, or community-college education, or university education, or whatever. They are so caught up in their specific work that they miss entirely the broad field around them, the changing world and its demands, which cannot be met merely by what they have to offer.

The center of educational gravity in society is shifting away from educational institutions toward informal learning, continuing education outside of school in the community, and self-learning without formal structures or conventional teachers. People in formal education need to take this revolution into account before it passes them by. Indeed, a recognition of shifting learning styles can help teachers improve their teaching and their outlook on the ends of learning by causing them, for example, to emphasize intellectual curiosity more and preestablished knowledge less.

It is obviously more difficult to change deeply entrenched attitudes than it is to add new programs on top of old. Partly because traditional educators have been sluggish to change, a vast smorgasbord of educational activity is now served outside formal educational institutions. There has been a Topsy-like growth of continuing education in business, the military, correspondence and proprietary schools, and the like, not to mention the extraordinary increase of continuing education courses and programs in universities, colleges, and public school systems. Little of this activity is reflected in the core of the academic world, which takes the lion's share of resources devoted to higher education and houses the strongest intellectual talent, holding presumably the greatest potential for improving all education.

It is commonplace to hear people say that Americans are sold on the value of education. What this means is that Americans have been sold on the value of core education, formal education for K-12, or K-16, or K-22, or whatever. The value of high school diplomas or college degrees can no longer be questioned. In a sense, educators have sold this system, the public has bought it (and demands more of it), and society is now stuck with it, whether it wants to be or not. Educators are in a position not unlike a manufacturer who stimulates the appetites of consumers for more of his product and then has belated qualms of conscience about whether the product is as good as he thought. He can improve the product, but in the practical order of things he cannot readily take it off the market. In education, the demand created for diplomas and degrees does not permit a reduction in their availability.

American educators should start moving toward a conciliation and articulation of core education and continuing education. On one side, we have a formal academic system that we support with public and private funds. On the other side is an informal structure that has grown up around the school and the campus, responding to people's needs for continuing education. Since schools and colleges can do only so much, and since lifelong learning is important, improved articulation is needed between what the schools and colleges do in the formal education system and what other learning situations and institutions can do to provide opportunities for continuous learning.

We must envision the broadest potential for the educational system—both formal and informal parts—and determine how and when learning opportunities can best be made available. Some things are more readily learned by adults than by youth; it is pointless to keep insisting that everything worth knowing has to be learned in school before one embarks on a career. The public should have a much wider range of choices and a much stronger voice in where and how learning opportunities are provided. A voucher system entitling everyone to a certain number of years of education whenever they are wanted would help. So would reducing reliance on degrees, with the aim of recognizing and rewarding competence wherever or however it is acquired.

At the same time we are morally obligated not to reduce the availability of the symbols of upward mobility—diplomas and degrees—to the less-advantaged groups in society. We forget at times that a youngster from the lower socioeconomic quartile, whatever his or her talent, has a much poorer chance of entering higher education than does a youngster in the top socioeconomic quartile (Cross, 1971, p. 7). Generations have been promised the rewards of middle-class affluence if they make it through the conventional, formal academic system. Opportunities must be increased for poor people to have the benefits of formal learning and the diplomas and degrees that go along with it. All this learning need not take place only in classrooms but also and importantly in careers, on the job, and in the pursuits of life.

Much is to be gained for education by a conciliation between core education and continuing education. At its best, education is a two-way system between teacher and student, as is readily demonstrated in continuing education for professional people. The practitioner has to take new knowledge, apply it, and come back to the professional school and say how effective it is, or how much progress is being made, whether he needs additional knowledge, and where the gaps are. He thus provides instant feedback which can help the learner himself, the educator in his research, and the teaching of preprofessional students. The same principle should be applied to the education of other students as well. This two-way exchange can provide a freshness and authenticity often lacking in conventional formal education.

The aim should be to build a new learning system that combines the intellectual vigor of the core academic system with the authenticity of life experience. Education should be easier to enter and exit from, with no penalty for remaining out of the program for one or more terms. Formal education should be better integrated with careers and made more accessible to adults, wherever they live or work, by using new technology, especially television. But old technology is important too. Books remain the best device for imparting knowledge; what the teacher must be able to do is to stimulate students to open them of their own free will. And the outcome is not only vocational, which is mainly stressed today, but also liberal and moral.

The social responsibility of the educator is as old as Plato and as new as today's citizen protesting local or national priorities. Can we, through lifelong learning for all, build a new and broader educational system that will give a deeper meaning to the quality of life and more urgency and wisdom to the amelioration of social needs? Society must ask instead a more important question: Can we afford not to do so? The learning system we already have is good, but it is not nearly good enough.

Patterns for Lifelong Learning addresses such questions as these by reporting on three separate though interrelated projects which have been carried out by each of the three of us. Part One deals with the second phase of an effort centered at the University of Notre Dame to outline in general terms the nature of a learning society and how to go about achieving it. Twelve recommendations from four task forces made up of distinguished national leaders are addressed to curricular and national and international policy. Part Two is an individual and personal essay by the second-named author on the relationship between continuing education and each of three important entities and processes: the academic community, the shaping of civic policy, and the creation of a new life style in the modern community. Thus this part contains a broadly philosophic analysis of some of the themes which underlie the more specific recommendations in the other two parts. Part Three moves directly to the question of how the general topics mentioned in the first two parts influence a specific institution, in this case Michigan State University.

We who have written and guided the development of this book have worked together in various relationships, only a few of which are noted in the book, and out of this common experience we have forged a mutual and sympathetic understanding of the great importance of creating a learning society in which the university has a continuing and vital role. The three institutions which we administer are different from one another, a fact which constantly confronts us as we discuss issues and practices. And yet we hope that they follow the same fundamental principles in serving their communities, distinctive though the nature of that service may be in each case.

It seems valuable to us to preserve this sense of both diversity and unity and therefore we do not try to coalesce the three parts into a single presentation. This decision gains even greater force from the fact that the first and third parts are the results of group collaboration, and we must remain true to the collective decisions of our collaborators. One consequence of this decision is that a completely systematic presentation of the entire topic is not to be expected. Our task and that of our collaborators is to dwell on the

Preface

issues of prime concern in this country at this time. A second consequence is some repetitiveness of content. A task force working in one study in one setting is likely to be impressed by the same crucial events as is another task force working in another study in a different setting. Yet each has its own point of view and something of value would be lost by any effort to force the two together or to choose one over the other.

We are grateful to many people who have helped make possible the studies on which this book is based; the names of many of them are listed in the Appendix. Here, however, we would like to express our gratitude to the staff and board members of the W. K. Kellogg Foundation for their financial and personal support in our undertakings. We would also like to mention several key leaders who helped to direct the project or draft the results. David C. Nichols helped greatly in shaping Parts One and Two, Thomas P. Bergin worked on Part One and William R. Wilkie and James David Harkness shared primary responsibility for Part Three. Russell G. Mawby, Robert E. Kinsinger, and Connie Polasky of the W. K. Kellogg Foundation and Cyril O. Houle of The University of Chicago provided good counsel in consolidating many aspects of all three documents. We owe a deep debt of gratitude to them and to their colleagues.

As already noted, each of us has had varying degrees of responsibility for one of the three parts of this book. In the first part, the writing is interwoven, often closely, from reports of committees and task forces. The second part is the work of a single author. The responsibility for the third part lies solely with the Lifelong Education Task Force of Michigan State University. The reader should not be deceived by this varied approach into the belief that we have been bystanders. Each of us has been directly involved in and deeply concerned about not only the separate parts for which we are individually responsible but also the interactive ventures which this book describes and which have brought it into being.

The aim of *Patterns of Lifelong Learning* is to suggest some basic changes needed to help move forward the concept of lifelong learning, perhaps the broadest and most useful concept yet advanced as a new and promising framework for educational policy planning. All we ask in inviting educators and the general public to read and consider these new themes is open-mindedness and the willingness to expand what education is today into something wider, broader, and more effective in a lifelong and often informal pattern for the future.

One might ask whether this is likely to happen, or whether the educational establishment is too wedded to the formal systems of education now in being. The answer should be that continuing education is happening today; it surprisingly encompasses larger numbers of students of all ages than the total number of young students in the formal educational system. The suggestion of this book, most fundamentally, is that education is one endeavor, and that it will have more coherence if those working in formal and informal education, in one-time and continuing education, plan and work together for a greater total and comprehensive educational impact on the people of this nation.

Notre Dame, Indiana   THEODORE M. HESBURGH, C.S.C.

Rochester, New York   PAUL A. MILLER

East Lansing, Michigan   CLIFTON R. WHARTON, JR.

September 1973

Contents

Contents

Patterns
for
Lifelong
Learning

A Report of Explorations
Supported by the
W. K. Kellogg Foundation

Part I

Continuing Education and the Future

The study "Continuing Education and the Future," was conducted through the Center for Continuing Education of the University of Notre Dame, with the support and encouragement of the W. K. Kellogg Foundation. The study was organized early in 1972 as an outcome of a national conference, "Continuing Education and the University," held at Notre Dame in January 1971, also with the aid of the foundation. Under the general guidance of a steering committee, the major work of the study was conducted by four task forces chosen to conform to the major themes of the earlier conference. (The mem-

1

bership of the steering committee and the task forces is given in the Appendix.) These task forces included twenty-four persons chosen from a variety of professions. Each group examined developments in its area of concern and recommended courses of action to improve the quality and accessibility of continuing education, measured against the national need.

The work of the task forces was carried out through a series of meetings, the preparation of position papers, and, in two instances, the holding of public hearings to solicit the views of interested citizens. Both the Task Force on Public Affairs and the Task Force on Social Responsibility conducted hearings in Washington, D.C.; the latter also conducted hearings in South Bend, Indiana. These hearings provided valuable insights and made all participants in the study more sensitive than before to the unfulfilled educational needs of adults. All of the work of the task forces was coordinated by Thomas P. Bergin, who conceived of the study and gave it general direction. The task forces director, David C. Nichols, drafted the reports of the four groups and the summary report of the whole study.

The rest of Part One, then, is based on separate reports prepared by each task force, on discussions with interested advocates and practitioners of lifelong learning, and on the views of the steering committee and the staff. A report such as this is a cooperative endeavor drawing upon the ideas of many people who do not always agree. Since this was true in this instance, the separate reports of the four task forces were integrated and rewritten as one report by retaining the substance but not necessarily the format, style, or details of the separate task force reports. Not all of the participants will agree with every statement made; however, every attempt has been made to express the principal concerns and points of view.

I

The Learning Society

$\mathbb{T}$he changing nature of our society requires virtually all citizens to gain new skills and intellectual orientations throughout their lives. Formal education of youth and young adults, once thought of as a vaccine that would prevent ignorance later in life, is now recognized as inadequate by itself to give people all the educational guidance they will need to last a lifetime. The obsolescence of knowledge, the rapid growth of new knowledge, the shifts in national priorities, the multiplication and complexity of social problems, and the close relationship between the application of knowledge and social progress all lead to the conclusion that lifelong learning is not only desirable but necessary.

Changes favorable to lifelong learning are not easily established. We have developed an educational system that is largely

3

oriented to youth and is poorly equipped to reach the needs of adults. There is a discontinuous relationship between learning and living accentuated by the persistent belief that education is preparatory to life and not continuous with life experience. The consequences of this discontinuity may be described abstractly as civic crises—urban blight, poverty amid affluence, racial and generational conflict. More concretely, discontinuous learning may cause an engineer to lose a career at age fifty, a new recipient of a doctoral degree to be unable to find a job relating to his or her training, second and third generations of poor people to be supported by public assistance because they can find no satisfactory way of gaining skills to enter the work force, or, if they are employed, no means to rise above a poverty-level income. We seem unable to apply skilled people and new knowledge very efficiently to the solution of some pressing problems; we have a glut of prepared teachers begging for jobs while many children are undereducated. During the past twenty years, studies have shown that new and potentially useful knowledge often languishes unused and that huge gaps exist between what could be and what actually is applied by professional and technical workers.

Something is clearly wrong in the way the society has conceived and structured the formal processes of learning. In the future, the United States should be conceived of as a learning society. Educational policy planning should begin with a comprehensive framework that addresses the needs of the entire population, from infancy through adulthood. The entire population should be seen as a national resource comprising a society in which continuous, purposeful learning is not only talked about but carried out in a great variety of settings and formats.

If the United States is to become a learning society, significant changes are necessary in attitudes toward the design of education. Terms like *continuing education* or *adult education* are too conventional and administrative in meaning to encompass the comprehensive responses called for in attitudes and national policy. The learning society is based on the concept of lifelong learning and refers to a universe of purposeful learning opportunities found both

4

within and outside the formal or *core*, academic systems. Stanley Moses (1971, p. 9) estimates that, by 1975, more than eighty million adults may be counted in a learning force outside the realm of traditional educational programs. Lifelong learning is thus a vast enterprise involving many millions of citizens who may never enter a college door or who may never return after once enrolling. And yet their needs are addressed only haphazardly in current national policy.

The increasing involvement of adults in furthering their learning is an encouraging sign. Unfortunately, the traditional educational system does not readily accommodate them. Peter Drucker (1969, p. 323) refers to an imminent conflict between extended schooling—conventional education for eighteen- to twenty-two-year olds—and continuing education. "If educators give any thought to the question, they assume that we should have both ever-extended schooling and continuing education. But the two are actually in opposition. Extended schooling assumes that we will cram more and more into the preparation for life and work. Continuing education assumes that school becomes integrated with life. Extended schooling still assumes that one can only learn before one becomes an adult. . . . Above all, extended schooling believes that the longer we keep the young away from work and life, the more they will have learned. Continuing education assumes, on the contrary, that the more experience in life and work people have, the more eager they will be to learn and the more capable they will be of learning."

It is not enough to argue the need for continuing education rather than ever-extended schooling. Even core education must reflect the fact that education involves far more than the classroom. As Moses (1971, p. 31) views it, "The challenge to public policy and educational planning is to support education and learning within the schooling system and elsewhere, wherever and however policy can aid in encouraging learning, realizing all the while the limitations and harm rendered by conceiving of education as coterminous with and coincidental to schooling."

In the learning society, formal education would be spread throughout one's lifetime. This reflects a recognition that people learn more readily when they see a clear need to do so, and also that some learning is more appropriate to one age than to another. It makes little difference where or how learning takes place, whether it occurs in the classroom or on a job, at age twenty, fifty, or seventy, as long as it does take place, and under circumstances appropriate to the learner. Education for adults as well as for children should be centered on the needs of the learner.

In a society that integrates formal learning with the stages of life, a majority of people between the ages of eighteen and twenty-five might be encouraged to consider alternatives outside the formal collegiate setting. For some, opportunities should be expanded in significant areas of national or community service, while others may choose to experiment with jobs, deciding eventually on careers. For this group of young people, the doors to college would not be forever closed; rather, the pressures to attend college immediately after high school would be reduced and the options kept open for any students to attend at a later time if they desire to do so. Increasing options is one of the key elements in a definition of education. The difficulties are legion for changing the national mind-set on college for everybody in the late teens. As a society we have succeeded only too well in selling the idea of extended schooling; yet we have only begun to think about the meaning of its near opposite, which is lifelong learning.

For those students who wish to enter postsecondary institutions immediately upon high school graduation, the emphasis on completing degrees in a lockstep should be reduced, with no stigma attached to stopping out for work or service experience and reentry at a later date. Appropriate credit would be given for such experience where applicable to degrees. The traditional reliance on the lecture-content method of teaching would be reduced, giving greater weight to individualized learning programs, on or off campus.

Continuing education for adults beyond age twenty-five holds somewhat different problems and opportunities. Education must be convenient, and it must be integrated with the pursuits of living—family life, careers, leisure-time activities, and the necessities imposed by active citizenship. While these compete for time, they

6

need not be barriers to further education; rather, all of these aspects of living stimulate additional learning needs which can be met, providing appropriate and attractive opportunities exist for individuals to participate in continuing education programs. These opportunities should be made available to adults throughout their lives as a necessary and desirable component of career, civic, and private life.

Institutionalized education has tended to promote the view that schooling is the same as education. As a result, we have become what some have called an overcredentialed society. Too many jobs require entering credentials out of all proportion to the skills needed to perform satisfactorily. The lockstep, traditional mode of formal education makes continuous learning unduly difficult, because in the past it has almost always been implicit that learning is both the province of formal educational institutions and of youth. In consequence, we have often burdened institutions with many indifferent students and have raised false expectations about what these institutions can effectively produce. This strain on both formal educational institutions and students would be reduced if lifelong learning were seen as the norm.

It should be recognized that responsibilities for continuous learning reside in all the major institutions of our society and at all levels of the formal educational system. What the school does is interdependent with what churches, families, employers, governments, and so on, do or do not do to reinforce the motivations and the opportunities for people to learn. The growth of new knowledge and its application can make the skills of a physician or engineer obsolete about as rapidly as those of a pick-and-shovel coal miner; readjustment and retraining is a shared responsibility among institutions. Under a system of lifelong learning, all institutions would share responsibility for helping people to educate themselves. Employers, for example, should give greater recognition than they do to the potential of the workplace as a prime site for vocational upgrading and personal fulfillment through well-designed educational programs. Church-related groups, families, labor unions, and the media all have unused potential for purposeful learning. In the future, all the major institutions of society should be conscious of their educational functions and take deliberate, planned steps to improve them.

Institutions are responding with programs to support the new learning styles emphasized by the need for lifelong learning. These programs of continuing education seem likely to experience rapid growth in the years ahead, without any substantial changes in national policy. As a matter of course, formal educational institutions will expand their offerings to accommodate an increasing demand for external degrees, individualized off-campus study, correspondence study programs, and other modes of reaching the varied interests of students. While this growth will be welcome and should be encouraged, much more has to be done. Educational means must be multiplied and made more accessible than is now the case.

The educational needs facing society are too great, however, to be challenged effectively by unilateral moves of only formal schooling systems or other institutions. Organization as well as attitude changes are needed to modify such contemporary problems as the acquisitive excesses in American life, the further pollution of the environment, the deterioration of cities, and the achievement of equal opportunity for all. Institutions are challenged to share the responsibilities of planning educational experiences that will improve mankind's ability to make decisions affecting the future and to avoid the catastrophic outcomes many scientists are predicting for an overpopulated, economically imbalanced planet. Education should become the responsibility of all components of organized society.

Professional educators have much to contribute to this leadership coalition. The colleges and universities offer prime locations and mechanisms for drawing people together, providing information, and guiding the organization of educational programs. Universities often take the lead in making critical analyses of problems and conducting the basic and applied research upon which decisions about the future developments of the society may be based.

Other essential functions are better carried out by institutions other than universities, although universities should encourage and support them. For example, our society has a special responsibility to help those who have been left uneducated or miseducated by the conventional educational systems. Universities have a direct influence through the education of teachers, citizens, and policymakers; and while subcollegiate institutions will have the main responsibility for reeducating persons failed by the schools, universities should be held accountable for their part, and acccordingly have a responsibility to lend their support and prestige to the development of effective continuing education and training programs for those who did not succeed in their earlier schooling. It is this sense of shared social responsibility that should bring institutions together in the learning society.

2

Curricula

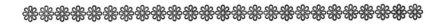

The future of continuing education and lifelong learning depends on basic changes in the core or undergraduate education of youth. In our complex society, job requirements are continually changing so that many employed persons must change their skills as often as five or more times during their working careers. Much undergraduate education, however, especially in technical fields of study, presumes permanence in career and competence. Major changes are therefore needed in undergraduate education since, from the standpoint of numbers, influence, and financial support, it currently comprises so much of higher education.

1. A substantial part of the university's undergraduate curriculum in every subject matter area should be redesigned to help students learn how to carry out a program of self-education and lifelong learning.

Many believe that a glaring weakness of our educational

system is its failure to inculcate a concern for and ability to participate in lifelong education. Educators stress the need by asserting that education must be a lifelong preoccupation, but this is not sufficient assurance that people will develop the capacity and eagerness to follow through. Much more is needed.

First, attitudes of teachers and students must change. While most conventional teachers have thought of themselves as the dispensers of preestablished knowledge and learning, the new situation requires a more cooperative relationship between student and teacher as they solve problems, discover knowledge, and learn how to learn. To say this is not to downgrade the role of the teacher; rather, it means that teachers should be educators and that learning is a shared experience between teachers and students. Students also learn while teaching others.

Second, the format of courses must be altered. The principal implication of preparation for lifelong education is that students must acquire the skills and techniques to help them know how to go on learning as long as they live. A great deal of independence must be generated in the learning process. The faculty members should be used as resources, just as the library, the laboratory, television tapes, programmed learning, and other resources are used. Students need to be involved not only in self-learning but also in groups, which is the way much of the work in life is performed.

The current move toward more flexible education and less reliance upon formal sequential training is easing the movement in and out of college, furthering work-study programs, and resulting in many more benefits. The association of eighteen- to twenty-two-year olds with mature adults engaged in continuing education can help to develop favorable attitudes of youth toward lifelong learning. Course content should reflect the growing concerns that education be both liberating and flexible. Problem-solving should be emphasized; resources available both in and out of the classroom should be used by the learner to analyze and cope with critical issues in his or her field of interest. Work-study, cooperative-education, and similar programs can help integrate formal education with career and community experience.

If undergraduate programs are infused with the spirit of lifelong learning, profound changes must be made in the objectives of courses and in the assessments of student proficiency at achieving those objectives. Much is made of student demands for less reliance on grades and formal examinations. If the learning experience is never ended, then grading for an understanding of a specific block of knowledge is not as important as assessing the student's ability to respond to changing demands made on his problem-solving facility. It is conceivable that in the interests of lifelong learning, one of the requirements for an undergraduate degree might be the student's ability to analyze issues or principles in areas entirely different from those in which he has had formal training. Examinations also can serve as starting points to help each student assess the effectiveness of his own study methods. Too often testing is seen as a mark of the conclusion of learning and not, as it should be, as part of the process of learning.

2. The responsibilities among institutions for inculcating skills and attitudes favoring lifelong learning differ according to institutional type and purpose; these different responsibilities should be recognized and appropriate steps taken to meet them.

Lifelong learning has different implications for curricula in different types of institutions. All educational institutions have a responsibility to develop in their students the ability to engage in self-learning, and to inculcate a spirit of intellectual curiosity leading to independent and purposeful lifelong learning. Because of the comparative selectivity of many colleges and universities and the substantial number of their students who aspire to professional roles, it is particularly pertinent for universities to help students acquire confidence in their ability to learn how to learn, often largely on their own.

For their part, community colleges and similar institutions may be fulfilling an appropriate role for their students by being technique- and content-centered, providing that students are adequately counseled in the implications of long-term changes in careers and vocations. These institutions also have recognized capabilities in providing continuing training in new careers for students who wish to change occupations or who wish updating in present careers. This is true as well for many other adult education programs sponsored by secondary school systems and vocational schools.

The society has a right to expect higher educational institutions to take a long view with respect to the consequences and implications of professional preparation. Never again should universities make massive efforts to increase the flow of trained personnel, as they did in the 1960s (in the preparation of teachers and engineers, to name only two groups), without at the same time seeing to it that the learning experiences are flexible enough to permit the absorption of any excess graduates so trained into related or complementary fields. Without the vigilance of concerned educators, however, the prognosis is not favorable, since ever more narrowing specialization seems to be endemic to the educational system. Moves toward more general education and core curricula should be encouraged.

It is well to reflect also on the fact that the kind of reorientation proposed here for undergraduate colleges, with the emphasis on independent and continuing learning, is consistent and compatible with the alterations that have already taken place in many high schools around the country. Changes in high school curricula to foster more student independence and self-direction have often been nullified by the highly directive and conventional programs which these students encounter later in colleges.

If lifelong educational endeavor must characterize the citizens of tomorrow, then they must be prepared for it today; and such preparation does not usually result from the current approach to undergraduate education. The undergraduate is poorly served, indeed, unless he has developed confidence in his own ability to be a self-learner and to participate effectively in the largely unstructured and unprogramed educational opportunities that lie ahead for him as a professional person or lay citizen.

3

Public
Policy

$\mathbf{W}$hen the able adult population of the nation is viewed as a vast learning force whose development is in the national interest, the basis for public policy becomes clearer. First, the provision of opportunities for lifelong learning has nationwide implications, since the development of human skill is closely related to the social and economic advancement of the entire country. The integration of learning with life and careers cannot be effectively accomplished on an ad hoc basis, dependent on the person's ability to pay, or solely upon self-interest. Rather, lifelong learning should be guided by public policies that encourage the systematic integration of learning opportunities with the needs of people at different stages of life.

Second, only through planned and implemented public

policies can socially and economically disadvantaged people have equal opportunity with other Americans to receive the benefits of the continuous education that will bring them a measure of career mobility. Cost, accessibility, and effectiveness of programs are major issues that concern a variety of institutions. In the absence of public policies that aim to revitalize the education of the poor or those who suffer other disadvantages, they will be permanently condemned by their poor schooling to dead-end, low-paying jobs. Obviously, education alone does not guarantee career mobility; there are difficult manpower issues involved that must be reckoned with by the society as a whole. Nevertheless, more effective education for the socially and economically disadvantaged people of society is needed.

To become a learning society, the United States must invest a considerable proportion of its resources in the education of all citizens on a continuing basis, at all educational levels, and for a variety of needs and motives including job training and retraining, education for more effective and enlightened citizenship, better use of the retirement years, and personal fulfillment. What is required to promote the learning society is a basic change in public philosophy toward lifelong learning. In particular, society should encourage a broadened role for the consumer in which each person has rights, as a citizen, to educational benefits and the freedom to select from among a broad area of continuing educational alternatives.

   3. The congress should enact a universal bill of educational rights that would guarantee to every citizen access to the widest possible educational opportunities.

The citizen could receive financial support at any age, up to and including retirement. The program should be accompanied by an income stipend to cover a portion of wages lost during absence from work to participate in education programs. It should also include a strong counseling program using imaginative new approaches. One suggestion, for example, is that in every community one cable television channel be reserved for two-way education and employment counseling, with the citizen using the telephone to ask questions of career counselors and educators who would refer him or her to the appropriate educational or employment opportunities in the community.

While this recommendation is universal and applicable to all citizens, special priority should be given to disadvantaged, especially low-income, people. Accordingly, any financial support made available might be based on a progressive scale reflecting the citizen's ability to pay.

Programs similar to the Universal Bill of Educational Rights are already operative in West Germany and France. The West German program makes it a right for every German to take up to two years of further education, with an income stipend of approximately 75 percent of the former wage, with an upper wage limit. This right exists for the employed as well as the unemployed.

People in the United States have generally taken the view that the education of people returns benefits to society in the form of increased productivity; the GI Bill of Rights is one example of the rightness of this view. It is time now to extend the idea by providing educational benefits to all Americans, young and old alike.

Whatever the specific format or method of funding, a Universal Bill of Educational Rights would be a strong step toward creating a system of lifelong learning in the United States, providing both vocational training and life enrichment. It would permit people to reenter educational and training institutions as a right and necessity, not as an appendage to formal schooling. Each person should be able to choose from among varied educational opportunities, in a flexible system that does not force him or her to give up the benefits should he or she leave the conventional, formal education system.

4. Changes are needed in public policies to promote lifelong learning through released time from employment, tax deductions or tax credits, and retraining programs that promise new careers. Public policy should encourage the use of school and college facilities for community education purposes.

16

Public Policy

Public policy should stimulate and encourage the practice of released time, in one's prime years, for pursuit of continuing education needs. For example, several hours per week might be offered to employees for this purpose and be considered an employee fringe benefit. The cost could be financed through the establishment of a trust fund fed by both employer and employee contributions. Employers should also be encouraged to match the education expenditures of their employees in much the same way that many employers match the college alumni donations of employees.

New possibilities of tax credits and tax deductions for individual education expenses should be studied; appropriate changes should be made in government taxing policies in the certainty that the treasury will eventually be repaid manyfold by more productive citizens.

Also needed to encourage lifelong learning, particularly for people with few skills, are cooperative employment training programs established by government agencies, private employers, and educational institutions. Employment opportunities should be made available to all enrollees who satisfactorily complete the training programs, with the involved government agencies, private employers, or the educational institutions providing the jobs.

Public policy should encourage the use of school and college facilities for community education purposes. The schools and colleges are one of the society's largest investments in real estate and facilities, and yet many buildings are used only a few hours each day, seldom year-round, and almost never on weekends. School and college facilities could be developed into community education centers with the entire community and persons of every age encouraged to use them. The Florida and Utah legislatures have passed measures encouraging community use of school facilities. In Flint, Michigan, the Mott Foundation has helped to make the school one of the focal points of community activity. In many other communities, steps are being taken in this direction, but much remains to be done before the schools become centers of community-wide learning. Moreover, it should be borne in mind that providing opportunities for people of all ages in the community is one way for educators to get public support for the schools at a time when bond issues and millage increases are being rejected.

5. Model programs of in-service education should be developed for public employees and elected officials.

The need for a realistic and comprehensive approach to continuous education in the public service has never been greater than it is now. If in-service education is to have the necessary impact on civil servants, who now comprise one-seventh of the labor force, it must be conceived as a management strategy for improving decision-making and a cost of doing public business.

The civil service, at local, state, and federal levels, should be a pacesetter for other employers. A given percentage of every applicable federal grant program might be specifically earmarked for training and upgrading administrative and other personnel. Such training should involve community leaders as well as the administering agencies.

The federal government has a particular opportunity to be a pacesetter in offering in-service education for its own employees. The Civil Service Commission already offers a great variety of such opportunities to thousands of civil servants each year. The Department of Defense has developed extensive opportunities for the education of military personnel. At the higher education level, about 230,000 servicemen and women are currently taking advantage of a program in which the Department of Defense pays 75 percent of the tuitions at the universities the service personnel select. The Graduate School of the U.S. Department of Agriculture also offers an extensive curriculum for federal employees.

These programs provide a rich resource of ideas and methods to test at state and local levels, where the concept of in-service education as a necessary ingredient of effective performance is only just beginning to be recognized. Elected officials, legislators, and their respective staffs should be provided with opportunities to deepen their understanding of public issues through educational seminars and other means. The recently enacted Intergovernmental Personnel Act offers federal assistance for training state and local personnel, but this is only the beginning, and state government policies are needed to promote in-service education.

Special programs must be tailored to fit the schedule of the busy executive, since it is especially difficult for officials in the most demanding jobs to take time off for study. In content, these programs should give high priority to building contacts between policy-makers and the "man in the street." Sensitivity to what is happening at the grass-roots level is a prerequisite for the effective functioning of modern government.

For employees in the lower grades, it is important that they be given time off to participate and be encouraged to do so through incentives that promise job upgrading.

4

Institutional
Initiatives

In the learning society, colleges and universities will have a leading responsibility for providing continuous educational opportunities. Until the 1940s, higher education in the United States was largely for a young elite; from 1945 to 1970, the pattern began to shift toward mass higher learning, although one which was still primarily youth-oriented. In the future, there will be strong moves to universal access to higher education for *all* adults, making available the resources of institutions to virtually all elements of society.

Meanwhile, stimulated in part by the turmoil of the 1960s, higher education is undergoing serious examination by those within its professional ranks as well as by concerned laymen and citizens. The nature and responsibilities of the university are being subjected to thoroughgoing review. Continuing education in the university, long a second-class function, has suddenly taken on new importance, challenging resident education and research, and competing vigorously for the resources to carry out its new responsibilities.

The university's responsibilities in lifelong learning include providing access to programs for students outside the full-time, residential pattern and also providing the inculcation of values and the development of skills in continuous learning for all students. Lifelong learning opportunities are needed in all phases of knowledge and the professions, and should be made available to serve the educational interests and changing careers of college graduates as well as those without degrees who want to gain new skills and lead more productive lives.

As important as the functions of the university are, the campus is not the only location for continuous education. New technology and the sheer volume of agencies and institutions supplying educational opportunities make it potentially possible for education of high quality to be universally available. The newest knowledge and the best teachers can be brought into factories and homes and into the most isolated communities through the use of television; indeed, every home can be a classroom. In cooperation with other institutions, the university should make educational opportunities available for all citizens everywhere.

Almost all institutions of higher learning and a vast variety of noncollegiate institutions offer some type of continuing education programs. No one institution can do everything, but each should affirm which part of the total responsibility it will assume. Ideally, institutional cooperation will replace competition and unnecessary duplication among programs. It is not unusual—indeed it is common—for several universities to offer similar continuing education programs in most of the larger towns and cities of the nation. Add to these the extensive programs offered by business and industry, professional and community groups, and the apparent duplication of effort becomes even more pronounced. Much more could be accomplished locally, regionally, and nationally by a serious combination of resources and by a collaboration of those agencies concerned with continuing education.

6. Consortia of institutions should be established on a local, regional, and national basis to pool resources for continuing education, with the aim of making sure that virtually all citizens have access to continuous learning of high quality.

As part of a consortium, institutions with interests in continuing education should study their present and potential institutional capacity and competence in continuing education, the needs of the local community or region, and the capacities and responsibilities of other institutions in the area. Different institutions have different clienteles, and therefore the contribution of each college and university to the total effort will be distinctive. For example, institutions with a community base may be more effective in pursuit of local needs than institutions whose clientele is national in scope. The aim of consortia will be to develop comprehensive patterns of continuing education to meet the needs of virtually all citizens.

Imaginative use should be made of cable television, correspondence study, cassettes, and other aids to learning. The human and physical resources of participating industries and agencies should be tapped, and the most highly skilled of their personnel should serve as adjunct faculty.

Local or regional plans should be designed, spelling out the roles of participating institutions. Such plans should take into account the contributions of the public school system, local business and industry, colleges and universities, and other public and private agencies with compatible aims.

The regional plan would assure that citizens have plentiful opportunities to earn credits toward degrees in a great variety of subjects, as well as an opportunity to enroll in a wide assortment of nondegree, noncredit programs. Flexibility of scheduling and ease of access should be stressed, along with the use of media, libraries, and other community resources, so that a broad spectrum of the community would be enabled to participate, wherever they live or work.

The plan should also include provisions that learning opportunities be made available not only for those who can afford to pay the registration fees, or who can take time off from ordinary pursuits to attend classes and seminars, but also for all those customarily left out—homemakers, employed women, minority groups, the poor. Every effort must be made to broaden the reach of continuing education programs so that virtually all interested citizens can participate.

The plan should also note special needs in continuing education for professions, civic leadership, citizen participation, and other areas of needed service.

As an incentive to the development of consortia, federal funding might be conditioned on demonstration of local coordination and cooperation. Special federal grants might also be made available to consortia for the development of model programs and new concepts in cooperative continuing education. Eventually, consortia might be accredited to offer credentials and degrees.

To help meet the needs of clientele in certain specialized areas, such as continuing education of professionals, special efforts are required. Professional societies, governmental agencies, and foundations, assisted by universities and other regional resources, should carefully determine what resources, public and private, educational and service, might be brought together in continuing educational consortia for professionals. Particular care should be paid to the need for linkages and feedback "loops" between practitioners and educators and between those involved in continuing education and those in universities and colleges engaged in basic professional education.

There is a difference of opinion about who the prime mover should be in national efforts to provide universal continuing education. Some have proposed the establishment of a national university, supported by the federal government. Others have urged that existing institutions provide the basis and framework for a national university, carrying out its functions on a decentralized local and regional basis. There have been suggestions for regional universities, which would consist of confederations of colleges and universities, educational organizations, and other appropriate groups pooling their resources for education, using television, radio, correspondence, films, libraries, theaters, museums, counseling centers, conferences, and seminars.

The consensus is that the appropriate public and private educational agencies should seriously study the implementation of these concepts on a regional as well as national basis, relating state and local continuing education programs to regional plans of development and relating the regional programs ultimately into the development of universal consortia truly nationwide in their scope and impact.

7. Each university should continuously renew its commitments as well as identify the resources necessary to meet its responsibility in lifelong learning. Account should be taken of the changing educational needs of groups to be served, and strong efforts should be made to improve access to programs.

Whether operating within or apart from consortia, all colleges and universities have responsibilities to promote lifelong learning. Colleges and universities should see to it that students of all ages are able to earn credits toward a degree in a variety of ways, including regular courses taught in the daytime or evening by regular or adjunct university faculty, examinations taken at various times, successful completion of telecourses, computer-assisted instruction, or independent study programs, correspondence, or other educational programs which an accredited college or university certifies as appropriate for application toward a degree.

In the 1960s and 1970s, there has been an increasingly rapid acceptance of the idea that students of any age can earn college credits or even a college degree. This concept and the education plans labeled "open university" or "university without walls" are promising developments. Any person, of any age or background, should have an opportunity to study a subject and earn college credit toward a degree. Residence on a campus should not be a prerequisite for credits or degrees.

Colleges and universities have been too rigid in their attitude toward accepting credits earned through continuing education, or, for that matter, credits earned in other universities. An accredited university program ought to be accepted for appropriate credit by all universities.

In addition to credit for regular courses, appropriate credits should be awarded for nonconventional, yet highly educational activities, including purposeful participation in voluntary community development programs or citizens' study and action groups. Universities should lead the way toward giving credentials for meaningful experience and competence, wherever these are gained. As possibilities increase for entry, exit, and reentry to formal education, there should be decreasing reliance on using predetermined courses of study as the basis for awarding degrees.

Continuing attention should also be given to the availability of noncredit programs. Many people who want to continue their education are not as interested in credit toward degrees as in the knowledge gained.

Many adults are independent learners; more can be attracted to continue their education by the adaptation of teaching and learning to their circumstances. Universities should lead in research on the independent learner and independent learning. Research on what motivates adults to learn and which materials teach a subject best should result in an expansion of educational opportunities to assist independent learning. Few educators believe any more that only full-time study can be serious, effective, and of high quality, or that schools and classrooms are the only environments within which adults can learn.

Changing educational needs should be taken account of, and strong efforts should be made to improve access to programs. It is obvious in higher education that all segments operate with limited resources. In most universities, educational programs are funded at less than optimum levels. Much research is needed, both basic and applied, and too few resources exist with which to carry out the work.

The general conception is that institutions of higher learning have enormous intellectual resources available to assist in providing alternative methods and approaches to solving social problems. As universities have increased in size, they have increased their involvement with government, business, organized labor, and other institutions. As the universities have become involved in the continuing education of diverse groups, requests for their services have multiplied.

Within the university, an administrative unit with responsibility for providing leadership will help to improve the probability of success of the continuing education programs. But also, excellence in a faculty member's efforts to promote lifelong learning should be rewarded by salary, tenure, academic rank, and sabbatical leaves comparable to those awarded to university personnel for excellence in research or graduate teaching.

8. Universities should find solutions for the pressing social and environmental problems of our time, together with increasing the educational services available for "marginal" groups.

The deterioration of cities, the impurity of the environment, the slowness with which ethnic equity is achieved, and other pressing problems call for assistance from the major institutions of the society. Universities already are trying to solve these problems by research and the attempts of talented people, but much more can be done.

Educators hold widely differing opinions about the most appropriate roles of colleges and universities in addressing the economic, political, and social problems of our time. These disagreements have been reflected in discussions by participants in this study. Some maintain that universities should be far more aggressive than they have been in seeking solutions to contemporary problems, committing their own resources and taking on some risks in the process. Others argue for a more conventional approach, stressing scholarly analysis of problems but disengagement from active implementation of solutions. These disagreements are inevitable and different institutions will respond in different ways. Nevertheless, there is considerable agreement on at least two points: that each university has responsibilities to address social problems, recognizing that some responses will be more activist than others; and that universities have responsibilities for helping to serve the needs of the rural and urban poor, the racial minorities, women, different ethnic groups, blue-collar workers. These responsibilities hold as much importance as continuing services to middle-class people, business and industry, the professions.

9. Efforts should be made to promote and improve continuing education for professional people through the use of special incentives. Retraining programs should be developed in areas of surplus manpower.

The principal purpose of continuing professional education is to help the practitioner maintain and improve his competence through continually updating his knowledge, skills, and attitudes. Since knowledge in some fields of work doubles approximately every fifteen years, this is no simple task. But this goal is of great practical importance in achieving a higher quality of life.

To improve continuing education for professionals, various incentives should be employed. Professional societies should require participation in continuing education programs as a condition for membership. Governmental service programs employing the talents of professionals should be required to show how continuing education will be carried out as an integral part of the program. Adequate budgetary support for continuing education should be made a condition for program approval.

Certification, licensure, or other sanctions applied by society to professional and technical workers should be based, to the extent feasible, on an objective demonstration of their competence. Any periodically applied sanctions, such as relicensure or certification, should be governed by the same general rules as the initial sanction and should relate to the demonstration of continued competence or acquisition of new knowledge or skills made necessary by advances in the field. The frequency of relicensure should be determined by the rate of development of new knowledge in a particular professional or technical field, as established by comparative analyses and assessments of the professions.

Special studies are needed to determine whether or not institutions, industries, and similar organizations, rather than individual practitioners, might be licensed as meeting standards of quality. The institution would then be required to maintain the performance quality of the practitioner, to monitor his continuing ability, and to guide him or her into effective remedial education programs if necessary.

Retraining programs should be developed in areas of surplus manpower. The expected continuation of a teacher oversupply and surpluses of professionals in other fields suggest an opportunity for a significant upgrading and redirection of key manpower. Every year, perhaps 10 percent of the nation's teachers could be enabled to return to advanced study on a full-time basis. (At the same time teacher training programs must be redesigned to make them more pertinent to lifelong learning needs.) Such retraining would permit teachers and others to move out of areas of oversupply and into areas of shortage, such as preschool education. Similarly, engineers might be retrained to go into ecological control.

The development of model retraining programs for highly skilled persons also offers an opportunity to experiment with new modes of experiential learning. Programs should attempt to embody approaches that enable the trainees to analze their own skills and to determine how these skills best apply to problems in the new fields of study.

10. Institutions should encourage the development of materials and educational programs in citizenship and consumer affairs for the use of a wide public audience.

The role of the citizen-consumer in civic life and in public policymaking is becoming a key element in new efforts toward social change. This role can be strengthened and enhanced through provision of education and training programs offered by a variety of educational institutions, namely, the universities and colleges, community colleges, public schools, and community service organizations. These programs and self-learning materials would aim to promote a better understanding of the rights and responsibilities of a citizen in the society. For some, much of this information would be presented on a how-to-do-it level: how to get speedier results from bureaucracies, how to participate in community-government programs, and how to make the most of the consumer role in civic affairs and community change.

Citizenship education typically provided by the public schools appears to be totally inadequate in giving citizens a grasp of effective participation in the processes of government. Among current issues important to all citizens are a better understanding of the statutory and discretionary powers of administrative agencies of government; an understanding of citizens' benefits in such programs as Medicare, unemployment compensation, veterans' assistance, Social Security, and the like; and even basic education about personal attitudes and actions that may lead to conflict between racial and class groups.

Education for effective citizenship is a lifelong process requiring constant updating. Such training should take place with the foreknowledge that information will increase the power of those people who have long been under-represented in the formulation of social policy, giving them tools to use against practitioners of prejudice and racism.

While drawing attention to the need to encourage continuing education in public policymaking by those who have been traditionally underrepresented, we do not wish to suggest overlooking such education for the rest of the population. Incentives to learn about effective citizenship are essential for many persons who, through apathy or lack of understanding, have ignored responsible participation in civic affairs.

11. The centers for continuing education associated with colleges and universities should assert new leadership in bringing resources to bear on new concepts and needs in lifelong learning.

There are more than a hundred centers for continuing education associated with colleges and universities. The current emphasis on lifelong learning implies that the strongest of these centers should exercise leadership and help implement the educational and administrative policies necessary to the achievement of the learning society. These centers can help to provide a focus for incorporating principles of lifelong learning into the curriculum, serve as a link between campus and community, and help to coordinate continuing education resources on a local and regional basis, to make sure that virtually all citizens have continuous learning opportunities.

It is not enough that the continuing education centers be conference and meeting places or glorified motels; rather, they should be concerned with educational planning and policies in a substantive sense.

As is true of their parent universities, continuing education centers cannot be all things to all people. Priorities of service are needed and should be made explicit. Administrators and faculty boards may devote substantial resources toward improving continuing learning opportunities for minority groups in the community. Others may focus on research and development in continuing education for the professions. Ideally, the strongest centers, including those that have in the past enjoyed financial support from the Kellogg Foundation, should work out a reasonable division of labor among themselves and serve as a national network, becoming pacesetters in new policies and practices on a local, national, and even international basis.

12.   There should be established a commission or center that would promote the aims of the learning society, based on the recommendations of this report.

Study groups sometimes stop short of suggesting ways of following through on implementation of their recommendations. In the case of lifelong learning, however, more is needed. While there is a genuine conviction on the part of educators and policymakers that continuous learning is essential in our society, translating this conviction into practice has been unusually difficult. Continuing education has been studied and restudied; a variety of groups has made recommendations. What is needed now is a center or commission, acting as an advocate, that would systematically pursue means of achieving appropriate responses from government agencies, colleges and universities, foundations, the business community, and independent organizations and agencies.

The new organizations should have a nationally representative advisory council and a strong staff. It should conduct or contract for policy studies on lifelong learning, and should emphasize implementation of the concepts of the learning society. Working with foundations and public and private agencies, it should locate resources to stimulate innovation in lifelong learning and follow through with appropriate actions in cooperation with existing organizations that have compatible aims. The new organization should have a short-term mandate of up to five years, and do everything possible in that time to work itself out of a job by helping permanent organizations to include greater concern for lifelong learning in their ongoing operations.

Part II

Universities and the Learning Society

5

The
Academics

The growing importance of continuing education to the goals of a learning society sharpens the question of how colleges and universities can best play their part. Virtually every aspect of American life has come under the influence of academic institutions—perhaps too much so. And yet advanced societies need knowledge to function, and the basic aim of the university is to create and share knowledge. Many of the great achievements, such as those in health, agriculture, public administration, industry, and communications, can be traced back to university classrooms and laboratories, where both ideas and talent are born. Modern universities have changed society and in the process have themselves been changed. Whether the university should provide even more services to society and risk transforming itself into a social action agency is the subject of vigorous debate. Almost without exception, the most provocative essays about higher education include this focus and provide fuel for a plethora of reformers.

Much of the debate has centered on concepts expressed by Clark Kerr in *The Uses of the University*. He sees the university as essential to the "knowledge industry of society," and, while many reforms are needed, the mutuality is proving to be of benefit to the partners. On the whole, Kerr is dispassionate about the trends, but forewarns greater care in designing the relationships. Later (1967), Kerr defines the need for a university devoted to an understanding of urban problems. He speaks of it as an "urban grant university" that would respond to the great national issue which the older university has not yet addressed.

In contrast, Jacques Barzun, among others, characteristically expresses concern that the university has become a service agency, exclaiming (1968, p. 6), "The American university has upheaved itself to 'catch up' and 'modernize,' words that mean: has ceased to be a sheltered spot for study only."

William Birenbaum sees it differently. He pleads for a new interdependence of city and university (1969, p. 48): "Government commissions and research staffs may become the backbones of future 'departments of political science' . . . and learning may become inextricably interwoven with and addressed to the day-to-day activities of the people."

These observers and many others have raised the question of how far the university can go in its service to society without overextending and weakening itself. Other concerns deal with how institutions can respond to the very changes they have helped induce, with fashioning knowledge for use in both the private and public life of the country, and with grafting change onto continuity. Advanced societies thrive by the ingestion of knowledge. Colleges and universities are the main centers for creating and sharing knowledge. How, then, may these interests and functions be connected? How do the connections concern the practice of continuing education?

Patterns for Lifelong Learning

Response to social need is not a new challenge for higher education. The social order has influenced it from the beginning. The medieval cathedral schools moved persistently from the preparation of professional clergy to the training of lay religious leaders. Paris, Bologna, and Oxford, among other European institutions, gained their differences from the ancient influence of the cathedral schools. As the princes and bishops began to prize the early universities, they granted academic freedom and autonomy. The advent of the industrial revolution, together with the recognition of natural science, moved science and technology into universities. The modern university reflects the incorporation of new needs by combining the devotion of Bologna to profession, the emphasis of Berlin on scientific research, the purposes of Zurich as the proving ground for the technologist, and the concentration of Oxford on preparing gentlemen and statesmen (Ashby, 1959).

In America, discontent with the elitist classical tradition created the land grant colleges. American students at Berlin brought home the ideas that formed Johns Hopkins and scattered broadly the concept of research as an important university mission. At the turn of the century, when economic development was an even greater theme, American universities expanded their interests to include many fields of professional study. The stamp of approval by the university was soon required before professional study was acceptable. Whole new types of colleges and institutes were created, culminating with the midtwentieth-century movement to build community colleges. The movement was inexorably one of increasing educational opportunity and attracting students to professions and vocations necessary to run the machinery of the industrial society.

Like the universities, adult education developed as a response to dominant needs expressed at different periods in the history of the United States. Some ideas were borrowed from abroad and adapted to American conditions. One of the best examples is general extension, which came from Great Britain in the 1880s, where the education of workers was recognized to be important. Courses for part-time students, largely adults, were begun by a few American universities, notably The University of Chicago. The University of

36

The Academics

Wisconsin is credited with introducing the idea of serving an entire state. From this heritage grew the present patterns of off-campus courses, discussion group programs, conferences and workshops, use of the mass media, correspondence courses, and other special efforts, including, since 1950, the great growth in residential continuing education, often in centers especially designed for that function.

Another important example of the changes in education inspired by social need is the Cooperative Agricultural Extension Service, sponsored by the land grant universities, the U.S. Department of Agriculture, and local government. Officially begun in 1914, Cooperative Extension answered the call of rural people wanting to improve farming practice. Through county agents, land grant colleges disseminated to farmers the results of agricultural research.

The university evening colleges grew from the depression years, which increased the awareness of the connection between employability and continued learning. Enabling people to work and study at the same time, the evening college served mature adults desirous of improving their employment status and encouraged the development of continuous in-service education for professional people.

In the second half of the twentieth century the primary invention relating to higher adult education is the community college. The community colleges add a vital new element to universal higher education. Within the decade of the seventies half of the high school students pursuing some form of postsecondary learning are expected to begin their study in community colleges, which now number more than a thousand. Of equal significance is the vast array of technical education and adult programs characterizing the approach of this lusty newcomer to education.

Almost from the beginning of the extension movement in the 1880s, its focus has been upon the utility of education for vocations. This shift from the self-development focus of classical studies to vocational studies is in sharp contrast to the writings about adult education which cling to the promise of self-learning on a continuous basis, with self-fulfillment as its end. E. C. Lindeman (1961, p. 5) expresses this view by observing that "adult education,

37

. . . accurately defined, begins where vocational education leaves off. Its purpose is to put meaning into the whole of life." This statement reflects contradiction between theory and practice. Lindeman's ideas, part of the liberal education tradition, have not fared very well in continuing education. Agricultural extension, for example, began with a concern about improving the family but moved later to an emphasis on the improvement of occupational skills. As universities devised extensions of themselves into the community, they too took up the thread of vocation: refined farming skills, professional in-service training, evening classes to upgrade chances for employment and promotion, and short courses for new careers. (Note the various classifications of the appeals to individual fulfillment in Cotton, *On Behalf of Adult Education,* 1968.) Vocational studies also promoted the interests of industry, which was able and willing to offer both economic and political support, a matter of no minor significance to the advancement of the land grant colleges.

During the past two decades continuing education has become a conduit for the transfer of knowledge from the campus to the community, where it is then applied to problem-solving. While an imperfect process at any level of application, this shift from individual learning for vocations to community problem-solving resulted from at least two trends in the world of higher education.

The first trend is the discovery of the federal government that colleges and universities are important centers in contemporary society for the creation and diffusion of knowledge. To stimulate production of talent and ideas for national needs, the government has fashioned an elaborate pattern of support to higher education. As the resources of the federal government are directed toward solution of social problems, institutions of higher learning have been drawn into many (perhaps too many) important government missions.

The second trend follows the widespread recognition that technological change is running ahead of the ability of social institutions to absorb the changes and serve the community more efficiently. Such issues as urban disorganization, racial discrimination, and environmental quality require better ways than now exist to evaluate policy alternatives as well as more effective interaction among organizations. As a result, community education programs are enlisted in the strategy to solve major social problems. Title I of the Higher Education Act of 1965 symbolizes the change taking place and links adult education activities ever more closely to "community service programs designed to assist in the solution of community problems in rural, urban, or suburban areas, with particular emphasis on urban and suburban problems."

These changes in the relationships of institutions to communities bring into sharp contrast the traditional elitist functions of universities. For two hundred years, colleges and universities emphasized the teaching of privileged students and the pursuit of scholarship. In the past three decades, higher education has joined the lower schools as an instrument of mass education, bending and altering standards to provide some degree of success to nearly every student, and developing programs of community (meaning *mass*) services.

This new role has disquieting consequences for both continuing education programs and parent institutions. As higher education expands into the community domain, the number of groups formed or stimulated to take an interest in educational performance increases. Community organizations, parents, employers, professions, and governmental agencies, although their interests differ markedly from the traditional education functions, must be heard and served by the imperfect processes of the academic world. Colleges and universities now find themselves strained under the demand that they intervene to correct the pathologies of society.

Educators inevitably confront the question of whether what they do off-campus is education or public service. It is, of course, both. Justifying their work as public service, however, tends to limit its assimilation into the normal efforts of colleges and universities. Educators are now considering how to broaden the definition of their teaching responsibility to include nonconventional, dispersed learning experiences for mature adults. In advocating this idea, J. McConnaughey asserts (1967, p. 170): "Teaching is teaching and learning is learning at any level and under any circumstances. If teaching is an accepted function of the university, then the extension of the teaching function to the larger community is a question of interpretation and not a third new university function."

Perhaps the first order of business in academic life is a thorough-going review of what colleges and universities can and cannot do in relation to societal needs. Patrons and constituents from the community should join in the conversation, in order that the community may better understand the purposes of the university and so that the university, in turn, may weigh the options available to it for community service. This discussion seems essential if colleges and universities are to avoid poorly conceived intervention strategies which assume that universities can help communities by "delivering" packages of information to government agencies, city hall, special-interest groups, or the planning commission. This assumed role of purveyor of knowledge implies that the university can serve as physician to society when it cannot.

The recent tendency to refer to *lifelong learning* or *continuing education* rather than *adult education* dramatizes the goals of the learning society. It is not easy, however, to design programs to achieve it. One difficulty is the separation of learning on the campus from education off the campus, the awkward gap between theoretical knowledge and practical implementation.

Continuing education programs are unlikely to be achieved until institutional leaders, including those in continuing education, develop ways of employing the community as part of the learning pattern of the college and university, thus reinforcing learning with experience. Students should have plentiful opportunities to learn in the community, just as adults should be encouraged to participate in campus programs. The traditional view of education preceding career should give way to a combination of learning and experience. Informality and flexibility would increase, and dogma about degrees, credits, time limits, and grades would diminish.

Continuing education programs should be related continuously to people's jobs and stages of life. For the university to be more effective in playing its part, imaginative reforms are needed in budgeting and administrative procedures. The traditional approach, tied closely to the formal instructional model for residential students, contributes to the neglect of off-campus learning. Administrators of adult education, trying to accommodate individuals and groups off the campus, face the complex task of matching community interests with faculty interests. Continuing education projects do not follow traditional patterns of academic organization, nor are they considered part of the teaching load or related salary and promotion systems. Administrators have to hire the regular faculty for off-campus teaching on an overload basis or recruit a separate faculty.

Continuing education fails to attain more status in higher education partly because some of its educators seek administrative or academic separation, even though continuing education is really an extension of teaching and research and no different from the main business of higher education.

Exclusiveness in organization is epitomized by the Cooperative Extension Service, which created its own corps of workers, distinct systems of personnel rewards and administrative nomenclature, and special forms of financial support. These innovations have at times alienated the host universities, despite the fact that the Cooperative Extension has an enviable esprit de corps rarely seen in academic life.

A few institutions, including Wisconsin and Rutgers, have established colleges of continuing education. Some institutions probably will continue to sponsor separate divisions of continuing education. Many universities, however, prefer to decentralize the continuing education function to the general faculty.

The choice between centralization or decentralization of continuing education is made all the more complex by the rapid increase of applied research and action institutes, many of which bear a relationship to community education. As the number of activities related to the community grow, new university officers are appointed to coordinate them. The complexity created will likely continue for a short term as continuing education enlarges its mission, decentralizes its function, and examines the relationship between the work of General Extension and Cooperative Extension. In the long term, however, the issue will likely become less important, simply because the continuing education function will become more universally sponsored, both by the faculty and by other organizations outside the university.

A commitment to continuing education will be more evident when it becomes a normal responsibility of the faculty and is incorporated into the general statement of institutional goals. This absorption will be hastened by the apparently growing emphases on independent study, cooperative education, work-study, and learning-service and the advancing recognition of the importance of learning how to learn.

Continuing education offers colleges and universities convenient ways of inviting students and local residents to discuss the contribution of the university to the cultural, professional, and practical needs of the community. Commissions on continuing education, consisting of faculty, students, and community representatives, are important educational ventures in their own right as they plan projects of mutual interest.

Effective management of community relations is necessary for university programs of continuing education. Most ties between university and community develop between particular departments and people of similar interests in the community, as between schools of commerce and businessmen and between schools of medicine and physicians. Nevertheless, ancillary specialists in curriculum, program planning, and counseling services are required. Few college faculties have experience in linking the needs of the community to the subject-matter departments of the university.

To broaden their concepts of teaching, members of the faculty should be encouraged to spend an occasional year or semester working on continuing education projects. Younger faculty members in particular may welcome such changes in their assignments. Moreover, with effective planning to meet community needs, the practice of extending teaching functions on an overload basis with its inherent implication of marginality will grow obsolete, and faculty should then receive fully as much recognition for their continuing education duties as they now do for research and under-graduate or graduate instruction.

42

The Academics

During the past decade, many new experiments with community organization have characterized the national search for better ways of providing social services. Public anxiety in a period of domestic turmoil stimulated the expansion of storefront centers, street academies, neighborhood services, and free universities. Such community organizations were devised to meet the needs of the disadvantaged minority and to provide guidance to all who are engaged in the search for human identity in urban society. It is to be hoped that the best of these new structures will survive and continue to improve the opportunities for learning in the community.

Some community organizations may possibly become distinctive urban centers of continuing education in their own right. Universities should encourage and support them. These centers would help adults learn through independent study, community participation, group problem-solving, recreation, and the arts. The advent of new adult learning centers could also offer citizens the opportunity to alternate periods of work with community service.

Future historians will see the years from 1945 to 1965 as a time of great public awakening about the social importance of universities. They may also point out the slowness of academic institutions to reach constituents long neglected by formal higher education, the unbridled competition and wasteful duplication among institutions, and the failure of colleges and universities to establish realistic institutional goals. It is no wonder that the general public is losing esteem for higher education, even as students are giving up their placid acceptance of the high school format and resisting the arrogation of their learning to the lockstep.

Academic leaders frequently respond to the situation in a tactical sense, often with the aim of politicizing the growing number of interested groups to gain support for their own colleges and universities. As we have seen, trustees, faculties, students, and administrators may hold markedly different views of academic goals. Administrators may lose touch with the quest for purpose within their institutions simply because they find it necessary to spend most of their time mediating among pressure groups competing for university resources. On the other hand, the faculty, their time consumed by disciplinary interests, may not understand the changing societal roles forced upon the university. On the whole, the disrepair within higher education reveals how little interest educators have in education about education.

To enlarge the understanding of education, scholars need to ponder the reconciliation of learning resources with public needs. Many laymen, even those who have never entered a college door, need to see the significance of academic freedom and excellence. Carefully planned forums must be devised to discuss policy alternatives in academic development. How to initiate these discussions, and how to keep them going, are special duties of the leaders of continuing education.

These mutual discussions are sometimes avoided because of faculty fears that this participation will weaken academic governance. But as greater numbers of citizens become more involved with higher education, they have growing interest in academic issues, whether or not they have more than an advisory role in policy-making. Whether this interest is viewed by educators as public relations or education is a choice of great importance in constructing the learning community. As educational opportunities become more widely available, the school and the college are likely to become more like community centers than they now are. At the higher level, the university may discover that a program of continuing education is much less the delivery of an educational service to a given clientele than it is the convening of citizens about critical societal issues, with the process and the impact, not the delivery, the aim of highest fidelity. Continuing education about societal issues and citizen participation is among the foremost challenges of the future.

6

Civic
Policies

The foregoing aspects of continuing education touch upon the nature of universities. Indeed, the roles of academic institutions in the future society will be strongly influenced by nontraditional programs for continuing learners. At the same time, community life will be interwoven with the functions of the university. Perhaps the most important relationship will be that between continuing education and citizenship.

Accordingly, a major task for educators today, one which has been long neglected, is education for civic competence. This task has not been taken up successfully by any part of the educational system. It is all the more imperative in the urban community. Says John Osman (1963, p. 20): "American higher education has been transmitting an antiurban intellectual tradition, and, unfortunately, has not been concerned with creating an urban one." E. I. Johnson, in outlining his view of urban continuing education, states (1966,

p. 292): "The great need now is for us (the universities) to engage all these (urban) bodies in a great civic dialogue about the long-range goals of our cities, individually and collectively, so that planning of a more comprehensive nature and at a higher level of excellence will guide the destinies of our cities and of the lives of the people in them."

These hopes are not being achieved. They are plaintive cries of frustration as man looks back upon his Earth from the moon and realizes his ignorance of good citizenship in an urban society.

Continuing educators have long hoped to secure support for urban needs comparable to the subsidy given to Cooperative Extension for agriculture. The anomaly, however, continues; agricultural extension services are free to consumers, while urban continuing education is pay-as-you-go. Title I of the Higher Education Act of 1965 was intended by the Congress to help correct this disparity. Unfortunately, this new legislation has done little, partly because annual appropriations have never risen to more than ten million dollars.

How to interpret the meaning of continuous learning in the urban society, and how to carry out significant educational activity to help accomplish it, are among the most serious educational challenges in American life. These tasks are decisive for these educators who believe that the new learning system should be based on helping youth learn how to learn on their own, rather than on professorial authority. Although educators everywhere recognize that formal schooling in the initial quarter of the life cycle will no longer suffice for the changes to be lived through in the course of a lifetime, they have so far been reluctant to alter their teaching styles to reflect this recognition.

One of the grievous lapses of public policy concerns the social costs and consequences which follow in the wake of technological innovation. A more efficient agriculture shoved aside those people who were no longer required to work its fields. These same people reappeared in pockets of poverty at the center of the large cities. The mechanical coal digger reduced the number of miners by half in a single decade, and the coal fields of Appalachia became a hinterland of human wastage. The diffusion of health science lengthens life but increases the pressures of population upon resources. Industrial processes which produce consumer goods also pollute and congest the environment. In the future, it is likely that increasing attention will be given to public policies that stress the human factors of technological change.

As man is freed more and more from manual and even administrative tasks, he can turn toward enhancing his own life and the lives of others. Helping people to do so is a basic duty of continuing education. The knowledge source for these new skills is suggested by the National Commission on Technology, Automation, and Economic Progress: "Much of this . . . technology will be derived from the social sciences and the humanities as well as the physical and biological sciences. It will be concerned with such values as individuality, diversity, and decentralization rather than conformity, massive organization, and concentration. It will seek to make work more meaningful rather than merely productive" (National Commission on Technology, Automation, and Economic Progress, 1966, p. 13).

In an era of systems, there should be more inventive consortia merging public objectives and pooling resources. A form of public management is needed to graft change onto continuity and to work through or around old political boundaries and ideologies. Helping people rise above such divisive symbols as rural and urban, private and public, liberal and conservative is necessary for the achievement of consensus about public policy. The genius of civic competence is to anticipate public needs and to translate them into public policy before the onset of crisis. Continuing learning has become the basic responsibility of the citizen and the policymakers and provides the impetus for the learning society. Not taking this responsibility shows the failure of public policy to anticipate the consequences of technological innovation.

Momentous changes are appearing in the nature of administration. Formal, authoritative, bureaucratic, and hierarchical models of management are being altered, in accord with the new themes of decentralization and participation in policy-making. The

47

alienation of students from central authority groups and the suspicion of many citizens that formal government has lost touch with the diversity of human needs are examples of attitudes promoting these changes. The administrative charts of large organizations, reforms in academic governance, and the widespread explorations with "participatory democracy" call for fresh ideas of organization which are not now expressed in formal administrative codes of procedure and delegation of powers.

The great and growing number of alternatives which modern society provides, together with the heightened awareness of man about his own needs, give emphasis to the need for collaboration and compromise between citizens and policymakers. The interdependence of knowledge, problems, and human talent suggests that groups of citizens devoted to resolving issues are often more sensitive to continuous changes than professional bureaucrats.

In a specializing society, the use of the term *community* frequently brings to mind relationships of space and time which no longer exist. A community is becoming only one among many centers of communication and transportation, fitting into much larger patterns of exchange. Citizens often give more attention to these patterns than they do to the more local "community." One author refers to the expanded version of community as the beginning of the "postcity age." M. M. Weber states (1968, p. 1097): "Only in the limited geographical, physical sense is any modern metropolis a discrete, unitary, identifiable phenomenon. At most, it is a localized node within the integrating international networks, finding its significant identity as contributor to the workings of that larger system."

At the same time, patterns of social transaction among cities lead them to an interdependence which often transcends national boundaries and policies. Satellite communications, the growth of official and tourist travel, international commerce, and the common characteristics of an international middle class all lend credence to the fact that people who live in cities, wherever they may be in the world, share an urban creed.

Higher education is intertwined with many national commitments—scientific research, mass education, and the alleviation of social need. All of these commitments link the federal government to higher education through expenditures of funds for specified purposes. Most universities have become national institutions in the sense that they foster national goals, primarily through research and mass education. Paradoxically, the *national* mood would now have universities make greater *local* commitments to public service and to helping their local communities. No single agency or institution is excused from the public demand that more be done about the disorganization, congestion, and pollution of cities. Meetings about higher education, if they are not consumed by discussion of student (or faculty) dissent, are sure to be dominated by appeals to academics to take up the unfinished tasks in cities.

While there is no dearth of opinions, university representatives remain uncertain about the exercise of the commitment to the modern urban community. Direct assistance may simply get in the way of the efforts of other agencies. Everybody agrees that the university has no business trying to build subways or to operate police departments. But when knowledge and talent are called for, the line between education and action is thin. The business of the university is to help people learn about the promise and the limits of civic life, assisting them with defining and analyzing needs rather than directly trying to alleviate them. And yet, helping people learn to make choices tempts the educator into undertaking planned social change, which is to a substantial degree a political process.

To what extent can universities help save the city? Like other institutions, universities are in turmoil over the proper way to answer this question. A certain anguish attends it: books roll daily from the presses; urban institutes spring from nowhere; and a misplaced comment can turn one into an urbanologist. The language is heated. What is wrong is more obvious than knowing what can be done about it. Universities tend to react opportunistically. They may allow the availability of grants to be more influential than reasoned judgments about institutional policy.

One may wonder if American universities have not gone far enough in their popular functions. Perhaps institutions other than

49

universities should have the mandate to service the community. This query emerges from the difficulty the university has in reconciling educational and service functions, and in responding to the numerous demands of constituents for more educational services of increasingly higher quality. In short, should the university deal directly with the community, or should it limit itself strictly to educational matters?

The question is not an either/or proposition. The university is involved with community problems whether it wants to be or not. Academic institutions will continue to maintain multiple connections with the community, and more are certain to develop. Some of these ties will be managed by interested faculty; others will depend on policy statements prepared by the institution as a whole. Many urban projects, while depending upon community cooperation, will be planned and executed by university personnel. University personnel will be relating to urban problems, undertaking research on urban living, providing consultant services to community groups, developing the campus into a cultural and conference center, devising special schools and institutes of urban affairs, and organizing special off-campus centers to extend resources from campus departments and schools.

Urban problems and opportunities require that many agencies and institutions cooperate in the use of knowledge to enhance community learning. Lifelong learning is obviously not the interest only of universities; many other organizations influence the total effort. University agencies of continuing education can provide leadership in this diversified setting, however, stimulating employers, unions, churches, and others to expand educational opportunity for their own constituents.

Citizenship implies competence in civic policies and professions. Education for citizenship cannot occur without reference to almost every agency and institution, both private and public. The university should cooperate rather than compete with other agencies and organizations better suited to servicing varied social needs. Each of these agencies can be viewed on its own merits as a center of learning.

7

The New
Life Style

Discussions of continuing education frequently give the impression that activities in the field serve the cause of society more than that of the individual. Fortunately, continuing education is now challenged by a new educational life style, one which demands that learning be not only vocational but also humanistic and personal. This new life style is person-oriented, not institution-oriented. It rejects the notion that formal learning is only for the young and replaces it with the belief that education is a lifelong process. It spurns the idea that higher learning takes place only on the campus and supplants it with the view that education belongs just as well to the offices, industrial plants, libraries, churches, and storefront centers of the community.

This new "nonsystem" of education sets aside the shibboleth that learning is accomplished primarily by formal study within regimented curricula and establishes the principle that education combines learning and doing, that it joins study with experience and service.

Replacing the institution-centered "system" of learning with a person-centered "nonsystem" is tantamount to revising the Ten Commandments. But in the decade of the seventies institutions and policies have been adopted that defy the time-honored procedures governing education and training during our lifetimes. These institutions and policies are already testaments to the awakening of institutions to the space-free, time-free realities of the new educational life style.

The new concept of education did not come about through the initiative of educators alone. Instead, it reflects some new realities and is a response to the turbulence in society—the shift from rural to urban patterns of living, the imbalance between social and technological invention, the growth of new knowledge and the obsolescence of old, and the mobility of the student. Technological change is so devastating to human competence that the monopolization of education by the young is insular, making continuous lifelong learning imperative. The disparity between the promise and the efficacy of education is so great that the enclosure of education within schools and colleges is ineffective, making communitywide educational activity essential. The expansion of the idea of education into a concept of lifelong human development is so pervasive that reliance on traditional methods is inefficient, making crucial a new mix of approaches to family, school, corporation and community.

Underlying these imperatives is a basic commitment to the search for personal identity by individuals and groups. This search is reflected in the odyssey of the bright high school graduate who travels for a year "to find himself," rather than entering college automatically as his counterpart of the fifties and sixties did. It is also reflected in the top-of-the-class law school graduate who sets up an office in a ghetto area, rather than joining a prestigious firm as his earlier counterpart did.

In a recent magazine article, the heir and owner of a small farm in New Hampshire describes his search for identity and the answer he found. Sent to Harvard University for a liberal education, he would wonder, as the crocuses began to spring up through the snow, whether his father had started plowing. He would then travel north, by subway, trolley, and finally by hitchhiking, until he reached the family farm. For, whenever he was away, he yearned to be back, to see what was going on. He finally realized that he was bound to the soil, so he walked away from Harvard Yard and enrolled at the agriculture campus of the University of New Hampshire. Today, he expresses the satisfaction of a person who has not only searched, but found: "I can't get my religion inside any concrete structure; I get it when the sun is coming up in the corn-fields and the dew is like pearls. It's not a humbling sort of experience at all. I stand full and proud and think, 'Man, you and I are going to make the corn grow.' " ("Three Hundred Years on the Same Piece of Land," 1971, pp. 44–53).

It is the challenge of education to help this search and to let the individual's own motivation, his own desire to learn and to grow, shape educational policy and educational activity.

Confronted by the demands of students of today, educators are responding with some imaginative approaches. Buoyed by the experience with cooperative work-study, study abroad, advanced placement, and independent study, educators are beginning to design new learning systems. These new systems stress learning at any place and time, emphasize credit for experience, work, and service as well as for study, and utilize new forms of educational technology as well as traditional instruction.

The idea of the external degree has come to the forefront, an idea that has the sponsorship of prestigious institutions such as the New York State Board of Regents, Empire State College of the State University of New York, the Open University in Great Britain, and the University Without Walls. These and other ventures

53

have been widely described in the literature of higher education (see especially Houle, 1973).

These are but a few of the pathways of the new learning system. Smoothing their progress are flexible approaches adopted throughout the nation: relaxed curriculum requirements, credit for community service, occupational experience, and interim-semester projects. These approaches seek to erase the dividing line between campus and community, accommodating students of many walks of life.

Traditionalists probably wonder why the dividing line between campus and community should be erased at all. A student during the depression years, gratified to have educational opportunity when so many went without, may have viewed the campus as a haven to prepare for better times and may want it to remain so. A student during the late forties, war-wearied and eager to sharpen his skills for the job market, may have viewed the campus as a port for job entry and may want it to remain so. A student during the fifties, determined to secure a set place in life, may have viewed the campus as a sanctuary for career development and may want it to continue.

In fact, higher education is caught between these traditional expectations and the demands of its constituents. Young students call for education that helps them relate formal course work to societal needs and search for solutions to societal problems. Middle-aged and older citizens call for new on-the-job arrangements in education that help them adapt to social and technological changes and gain means of influencing future changes. Disadvantaged persons call for equal opportunities in education that help them improve their knowledge and skills and reach the mainstream of society. These constituents, indeed the public as a whole, will not let the campus remain a haven or a sanctuary. Instead, the population, through national consensus and government policy, looks to higher education for ideas and talent in solving urban problems, for assistance in balancing social and technological solutions, and for help in overcoming confusion and discord.

Slowly, but positively, education has accepted the challenge, as it has joined with government, industry, and other segments of the community in cooperative efforts such as the continuing-education curricula, the programs for the disadvantaged, the training of persons to help underdeveloped countries, and the fundamental and applied research. Higher education is beginning to abandon its traditional unilateral function for multilateral approaches more responsive to the human hopes and needs of the learning society.

The campus and community are now required to reach mutual purposes on objectives and approaches, plan cooperatively, carry on joint programs, organize interdependent curricula, share facilities, and use communications technology. Rather than being peripheral, as a client receiving fringe benefits and services, the community should serve as a learning center for educational organizations and institutions, and citizens should participate as advisors in all phases of education and training activity, from planning to achievement.

External degrees, colleges without campuses, industrial training centers, open universities, school without walls, and new consortia are attempts to achieve this crucial cooperation. Thus a man who has worked for the local gas company will prove his knowledge and skills by passing a series of examinations, and receive a degree in business administration, opening the doors to a supervisory position. A housewife who has raised three children will be enabled to find a second career as her children go away to make their own careers. An inmate in prison who formerly had no hope will have an opportunity to rehabilitate himself through a planned educational program that leads to a job with a future. A young man enrolled in a prestigious liberal arts college will stop out for a year to work with a consumer welfare agency and will receive credits for doing so toward his degree in political science.

The new flexibility of higher education will make it possible for these opportunities to multiply. People-centered education means that institutions will adapt programs to meet needs and opportunities wherever they exist in the community, rather than expecting the community to come to the campus.

Faculties who teach the "new" students will also change.

The "new" teacher will guide rather than lecture, helping the student to self-discovery of knowledge. Rote learning will be replaced by experimentation, with emphasis on individualized reading and self-teaching. The best teachers have always known the joy of watching a student discover truth for himself, rather than having it handed to him as a book of rules. This teacher and this style of learning, will be sought by the new system.

Above all, the advent of the learning society gives people virtually unlimited opportunities for purposeful learning. And although educational institutions must expand opportunities, it is ultimately the student's responsibility to educate himself. This is an ancient principle, perhaps, but one that has often been lost sight of in a society that too often expects formal educational institutions to do all the providing. Thus the new life style is in some respects an old life style rediscovered. It is a quest for moral, intellectual, physical, and economic individual fulfillment, in the best sense of a liberal education. This is what lifelong learning means, and it is one of the aims of the learning society.

Part III

The Lifelong University

For decades most people have spoken of education as a process focused upon the development of skills and attitudes within formal K-12 school systems and campus-based postsecondary institutions. Today, however, as has been pointed out in Part Two, societal conditions demand expanded access to learning resources over greatly extended periods of time, in all likelihood throughout the entire course of our lives. Among educators a growing realization of the benefits of lifelong education has led to major planning projects across the United States, one of the most recent of which has been the Notre Dame Study on Con-

Reprinted with modifications from *The Life-Long University,* © 1973 by the Board of Trustees, Michigan State University, East Lansing.

tinuing Education and the Future, whose conclusions have been reported in Part One.

The Notre Dame Task Forces and similar commissions have assessed the issue of lifelong education in a primarily national context. Responses are required within many types of individual institutions, among them corporations, governmental and civil service units, primary and secondary schools, community colleges, vocational and technical schools, and universities. Each institution must find answers to specific questions. What capacities does the institution possess for lifelong education? How can its financial and manpower resources support lifelong educational activities? What organizational modifications, if any, are required to enhance lifelong educational involvement? Perhaps most important, how can the institution forge a cooperative role in a "lifelong educational system" made up of many different kinds of social entities?

Even as the Study on Continuing Education and the Future progressed, Michigan State University initiated its own institutional inquiry. In a report published in November 1971, a university-level planning body, the Commission on Admissions and Student Body Composition, recognized the importance of lifelong education, suggesting the creation of a presidential commission to recommend a future role for Michigan State University. In February 1972, the president created a Task Force on Lifelong Education. (The names of the members of the Task Force are given in the Appendix.) The Task Force met for a year before issuing its final report, *The Lifelong University*, published on the East Lansing campus in April 1973. The substance of that report is found on the following pages.

The Task Force was charged with the following formal responsibilities:

(1) To develop for Michigan State University, a definition of *lifelong education* that reflects a set of philosophical and specific program objectives.

(2) To identify the nature of the program (formal, informal, mixed), a strategy for implementation, and the institutional arrangements necessary to reach specific lifelong-education participants.

The Lifelong University

(3) On the basis of a program model, design an organizational structure specifically for Michigan State University which insures: (a) a lifelong educational component that is soundly and fully integrated into the structure of the university; (b) a means for refocusing and marshaling present institutional resources to facilitate lifelong education; (c) the development of a faculty-staff reward system which puts lifelong education in perspective with other primary functions of the university.

(4) Finally, recognizing that Michigan State University cannot alone meet all the needs of lifelong education in the state of Michigan or elsewhere, the Task Force will examine other external relationships, particularly the following three: (a) the university's role and relationship in a statewide lifelong educational system, including but not limited to external degree programs; (b) the share of the total burden in lifelong education which the university should undertake, based upon its unique resources and comparative advantages; (c) the programmatic opportunities for cooperative efforts with the growing private educational industry.

Although a philosophical commitment to lifelong education is gaining ever greater acceptance, the charge to the Task Force on Lifelong Education was unique: it conducted an examination and analysis of responses, innovations, and restructuring necessary to implement lifelong education as an ongoing component of that institution.

Members of the Task Force soon found that the connotations of lifelong education varied widely from person to person. After extensive discussion and public debate, the following definition was adopted:

"For the individual, lifelong education is a process of learning that continues throughout life. Lifelong education implies an opportunity—and for some, an obligation—to seek knowledge which contributes to personal growth and to the welfare of society.

"For institutions of higher learning, lifelong education is a process of academic instruction at postsecondary levels and of educational service to individuals and institutions at many levels of need. Lifelong education implies for all colleges and universities a responsibility to recognize, anticipate, and assist in meeting the needs of individuals and groups.

"Lifelong education, then, includes both the individual's process of lifelong learning and the institution's process of lifelong service, insofar as these processes are appropriate to the mission and available resources of that institution."

Going beyond the definition, it is important to recognize that lifelong education is one aspect of a broad pattern of reform throughout higher education not only in this country but also across the world. Other parts of the pattern include heightened interest in nonformal approaches to learning, revisions in financial and administrative practices, expanded accessibility to new or underrepresented audiences, educational technology, and interinstitutional cooperation. As preceding and subsequent pages demonstrate, these elements are not easily separated; each holds implications for the others. The pattern, moreover, is not exclusive to postsecondary education; similar processes can be detected at work in primary and secondary school systems. Taken together, reform and innovation seem to be shaping education into a more effective and responsive social instrument.

The Task Force on Lifelong Education began its investigation as part of an ongoing, multidimensional process of institutional change. The members realized that the university's role in lifelong education would be influenced by its responsibilities in other areas, by unusually restrictive legislative fiscal policies, and by the anathema of all planning projects—the fluidity of societal conditions. Accordingly, the Task Force sought to balance speculation and planning with an awareness of the complexity of issues and a recognition of the realities of circumstances which constrain the university.

The Task Force realized the need for colleges and departments of the university to retain their delegated initiative and responsibility in relation to academic activities. In addition, the Task Force was intrigued by the concept of recommendations which not only considered changing societal conditions but used such forces constructively. For these and other reasons, the Task Force generally did not identify specific audiences, design programs for them, or assign programs to particular academic units. Instead, its report attempts to focus upon a *process* which could respond to evolving circumstances while focusing on the goal of integrating lifelong education into the regular activities of faculty and staff.

The Task Force members, a cross section of the university community, included three deans, six faculty members, three students, four senior academic administrators, two alumni, and three representatives from the wider community. William R. Wilkie, assistant to the university president, served as chairman of the Task Force; James David Harkness, editorial consultant, prepared the final report and coordinated its original publication at Michigan State University.

The Task Force conducted many meetings both on and off the campus and consulted with a wide range of people in the university and outside it. At least 151 individuals were consulted, some of them more than once. Meetings were held with many campus groups, such as the advisory councils of the various colleges and the Council of Graduate Students. Perhaps no individual institutional study has ever used so broad a base of consultation in its effort to establish guidelines for the future.

The Task Force soon realized that Michigan State University must seek an appropriate role in a coordinated lifelong educational system composed of a variety of social and educational institutions. Whether relationships within this system are voluntary, contractual, or established by legislative act, all participating institutions must recognize the requirements and contributions of those with which they must cooperate.

8

Lifelong Education: Traditions and Commitments

Michigan State University serves the people of the state through teaching, research, and those activities often called public service. In seeking to fulfill this broad charge, the university provides both undergraduate and graduate-professional curricula. Seventeen colleges offer programs in more than 471 fields. More than ninety-five hundred degrees, including some six hundred doctorates, are awarded each year. A faculty of more than thirty-one hundred supports this diverse instructional effort.

Michigan State University also conducts both basic and applied research of local, state, national, and international significance,

Lifelong Education: Traditional and Commitments

supported by approximately twenty-seven million dollars in annual funds. In addition, ten million dollars in federal, state, and private appropriations maintain more than four hundred agricultural experiment station projects in twenty-seven university departments. Altogether, these resources undergird investigations in educational psychology, geology, computer science, ecology, biomedical science, sociology, political science, physics, and a host of other areas.

Growing out of more than a century of experience, Michigan State University's commitment to lifelong education is an integral part of its present operation. The best-known vehicles for the dissemination of knowledge beyond the campus are the Cooperative Extension Service and the Continuing Education Service. Cooperative Extension provides programs in agricultural production, marketing, family living, and resource development, as well as the 4-H youth program. A recent major effort has been the expansion of nutrition programs for low-income families. Extension field agents and volunteer leaders serve all eighty-three Michigan counties, supported by on-campus scientists and specialists in seven of the colleges of the university.

The Continuing Education Service annually offers more than twelve hundred credit and noncredit courses in eighty-five Michigan communities. The Evening College, based on the East Lansing campus, enrolls more than four thousand students each year in 150 different courses. In addition, the Continuing Education Service conducts one of the largest conference programs in the nation, partially at the Kellogg Center for Continuing Education. Each year nearly fifty thousand adults attend educational meetings at the Kellogg Center and at other locations throughout the state. Finally, the Continuing Education Service maintains the educational broadcasting facilities of the University—WKAR, WKAR-FM, and WKAR-TV.

Other units of the university are equally concerned with lifelong education. The School of Labor and Industrial Relations—created in 1956—provides educational opportunities aimed at fostering self-improvement among individual workers, public and private managers, and public employees involved in implementing manpower programs. The Center for Urban Affairs has launched an urban extension program, carrying the land grant heritage into the heart of the modern city. And, indeed, every college of the university provides varying educational opportunities to citizens beyond the campus.

Michigan State University's past and present commitments, the Task Force realized, held a two fold significance. First, they provided a reservoir of experience and expertise from which future efforts could draw. Second, they were exemplary of the involvements of many land-grant institutions in meeting adult educational needs. Thus, the investigations of the Michigan State University Task Force had ramifications for the specific institution *and* many similar colleges and universities.

In its initial assumptions, the Task Force on Lifelong Education affirmed the historic and present missions of the university: *(a) The university is currently engaged in a critically important mission for society in carrying on the education of on-campus graduate and and undergraduate students in degree programs and the conduct of research. It will continue to perform these functions into the indefinite future. (b) Because of its history as a land grant institution and its tradition of public service, Michigan State University is in a unique position to help extend lifelong education opportunities to the citizens of the state.* (Assumptions which undergird the whole study are given in italics throughout Part Three.)

In order to realize its institutional potential for lifelong education, Michigan State University must now expand its present objectives, especially in areas of public service. The Task Force on Lifelong Education formulated the following statement of mission as a guideline for this expansion.

"For Michigan State University, lifelong education implies a responsibility to foster commitment to lifelong education among its students and audiences and to aid them in developing self-learning motivation and skills; an increased sensitivity to the educational needs of the citizens of Michigan and a dedication to removing barriers to educational opportunity; a responsibility to apply its appropriate knowledge, expertise, and research capacities to assist in solving problems central to lifelong education; a responsibility to continue and expand the availability of institutional resources for community problem-solving; an examination of existing interinstitutional relationships and, wherever appropriate, the creation of new ones."

In establishing the objectives central to the expansion of Michigan State University's role in lifelong education, the Task Force was guided by several of its assumptions. Some required no modification; others, influenced by new data and discussions, needed refinement to ensure supportability. Formally stated, the relevant assumptions are as follows: *(c) The educational needs of a large segment of our present population are not now met by the existing formal educational system. (d) A lifelong educational system should include formal and nonformal programs, credit and noncredit programs, on- and off-campus programs, and problem-focused public service programs. (e) If adequate educational opportunities and appropriate arrangements are provided on the Michigan State University campus, a large number of students, professionals, and others will commute to take advantage of them. (f) There is a significant need for educational opportunities at the local level for citizens who, because of work schedules, geographic locations, or responsibilities in the home, cannot commute to the university campus. (g) If adequate educational opportunities exist at the local level, many students will elect to do at least part of their undergraduate work, and perhaps their graduate work as well, close to home, in some cases sandwiching their education with careers or on-the-job training. (h) If adequate educational opportunities are easily accessible at the local level, professional workers will take advantage of them to improve and update their skills. (i) Because of the large potential audience and the limited resources, any system to reach large numbers of people in the state will have to incorporate instructional technology and independent study. (j) Any system for providing lifelong education must serve a heterogeneous population which has special and unique requirements for counseling, tutoring, and other auxiliary services supporting the academic effort. (k) In addition to present degrees, a wider variety of certification procedures and cer-*

tificates are needed to verify student competencies and to reward en route achievement in lifelong education.

The Task Force organized the recommendations derived from these assumptions into three broad categories: (1) modification of existing procedures, (2) modification of existing programs, and (3) new programs. The categories were constructed to reflect the extent of manpower and economic resources necessary to implement recommendations subsumed within them. The Task Force felt that the university could begin quickly and inexpensively to expand its role in lifelong education by modifying many of its policies and procedures. Changing existing programs or initiating new ones, on the other hand, might cost more and take longer.

Classification, of course, was not always simple. Many recommendations refused to fit neatly into any single category, while others seemed to fall under two or even all of the headings. (For the purpose of clarification, distinctions were made among participants in educational programs according to the following system: learners were referred to as either *conventional*—presently served by the university through regularly scheduled campus courses—or *nonconventional*—requiring innovative formats not necessarily directed toward the awarding of a degree. Conventional learners may be either *residential*—living in university housing—or *nonresidential*. Nonconventional learners may be either *commuters*—participating in learning experiences offered on campus—or *off-campus participants*. The conventional learner is usually the more traditional "student"—young, degree-oriented, and engaged in university attendance as a primary activity, while the nonconventional learner is usually older and engaged in education as one of many important involvements.)

9

Modification of
Existing Procedures

$\mathbf{M}$any administrative and
academic-administrative procedures, having evolved in a context
shaped largely by the needs of conventional students, now present
untoward difficulties to the non-conventional student. In order to
serve the participant who wishes to take classes at night, off-campus,
in non-degree formats, and so on, these procedures require modification. The Task Force felt that the modification of existing procedures could be achieved more quickly than the modification or
creation of programs themselves; thus, the report turns first to
procedural adjustment.

Admissions

Through its present admissions procedures the university
strives to assess each applicant on an individual basis. This evaluation is done according to the applicant's past academic performance

(usually documented by high school records, general equivalency diplomas, or college transcripts), his entrance examination scores (on the American College Test or Scholastic Aptitude Tests), letters of recommendation, and personal interviews.

In practice, transcripts and examination scores carry by far the greatest influence. For older applicants, however, the years and circumstances intervening between their last formal education and admission to the university may require criteria that do not concentrate heavily on past academic performance.

1. Michigan State University should continue to expand admissions criteria to reflect more adequately an applicant's ability to participate successfully in university-level educational experiences. Criteria should include personal maturity, motivation, independence, career performance, and previous life experience, including academic background. [The recommendations are given in numerical order throughout Part Three.]

The work and recommendations of the Commission on Admissions and Student Body Composition should serve as a foundation for the implementation of this recommendation.

Registration

The size, complexity, and record-keeping obligations of Michigan State University make enrollment and registration procedures somewhat ponderous. The university is presently investigating ways to enroll and register its current students with greater efficiency and convenience than at present, and the Task Force on Lifelong Education endorses this effort. Alternative enrollment and registration procedures may be only an inconvenience to young adults but because of his location, career and family responsibilities may exclude the older adult from educational participation.

2. The university should undertake the provision of new enrollment and registration options designed to facilitate entry and ongoing participation by the nonconventional student.

68

Modification of Existing Procedures

Examples of possible innovations include but are not limited to enrollment and registration by mail; enrollment and registration by telephone; preserving sections or portions of sections, especially in night or weekend courses, for nonconventional students; separate enrollment and registration for nonconventional students at times convenient for them.

3. Although nonconventional students may require special enrollment and registration arrangements, the university should minimize segregation by age in the classroom or elsewhere, insofar as this is compatible with the limitations imposed by location, work schedules, or family obligations.

Orientation

Undergraduate students newly admitted to the university must participate in an orientation program before enrolling for their first term of classes. At orientation, the student becomes acquainted with the campus, takes placement tests, talks to advisors, and chooses classes. The nonconventional student needs a special set of orientation experiences. For participants pursuing their education off campus, for example, a knowledge of the East Lansing campus is at best incidental, while a briefing on the advantages and disadvantages of independent study may be indispensable.

4. The university should initiate at least one separate orientation program designed around the special conditions under which nonconventional students participate in university programs.

Although separate, this orientation program should attempt to acclimate and inform nonconventional students regarding the full range of university programs and activities, perhaps by visiting traditional classes and making use of conventional students as resource persons. The orientation program should not be mandatory; if orientation constitutes an unreasonable inconvenience for some participants, complementary printed orientation materials should be distributed.

Transfer of Credits

Although Michigan State University will accept any number of undergraduate transfer credits, baccalaureate degree requirements dictate that at least forty-five credits be earned in courses given by the university. Generally these credits are gained during the final year of attendance, although fifteen of the last forty-five credits can be transferred from other institutions if the student will have the required number of Michigan State University's credits upon graduation. Master's candidates are allowed twelve transfer credits, while a committee determines the number of transfer credits acceptable for a doctoral candidate.

Many individual situations arise that require adaptation of current rules for transfer of credit. Requiring that thirty to forty-five senior credits be earned at Michigan State University creates a hardship for the person who has attended the university for ten full terms (or part-time equivalents) and who, for reasons beyond his control, must move to another area to complete a degree. On the other hand, many successful students from other accredited colleges and universities must, late in their senior year, move to the East Lansing area for reasons beyond their control. If institutions are fully accredited, it may be unnecessary to question transferability of credits at any given level. Specific degree requirements can be maintained or adjusted for nonconventional students by individual departments and colleges.

5. The university should continue to examine its credit transfer policies and develop increased flexibility especially in meeting the individual needs of nonconventional students.

Scheduling

The regular eight-to-five, Monday-through-Friday schedule of university operations is manifestly inconvenient for many nonconventional participants, both those who commute to campus and those involved in off-campus learning experiences. Work schedules and family responsibilities may leave only nights and weekends for the pursuit of educational goals. Although the university does offer a variety of learning experiences at night, it is difficult and often impossible to complete an undergraduate degree program without daytime attendance.

6. *The university should design and put into effect a more flexible academic schedule on and off campus, making both degree and nondegree programs available at night and on weekends.*

7. *Appropriate advisory and administrative services of the university should be available at night and on weekends to accommodate nonconventional participants engaged in programs offered during those times.*

Both academic and administrative flexibility should be achieved primarily by rescheduling rather than expanding offerings and services. For those who enter degree programs other than at the beginning of fall term, progress may be hindered by difficulties encountered in obtaining prerequisites, enrolling in courses out of sequence, and so on. The university should diversify sequence schedules of course availability in order to respond more effectively than it now does to participants who enter during summer, spring, and winter quarters.

8. *The university should investigate ways to more usefully employ summer quarter—for example, by providing brief residential sessions for adults and their families.*

Time Limitations for Degrees

There is no time limit for completion of the baccalaureate degrees offered by Michigan State University. In most academic units, the time limit for completion of master's degree requirements

71

is five calendar years. Doctoral students must take comprehensive examinations within five years after their first enrollment in the doctoral program, and they must complete dissertations and other requirements within eight years of that date.

The value of time limits for degrees is dependent upon the nature of each discipline and the level of study undertaken. The Carnegie Commission on Higher Education has suggested that many degree programs, especially below the doctoral curriculum, could be completed in less time than is now normal. Conversely, many adults who must pursue their degrees on a part-time basis will require longer periods than students who are enrolled full time. The speed with which knowledge is revised and expanded (especially in certain scientific and professional fields) also requires time considerations.

9. Time options for the completion of degree requirements should be expanded according to criteria based on the type and level of degree involved, the audiences who seek that degree, and the extent of disciplinary flux. This expansion should be the responsibility of the academic units of the university.

Enrollment Options

Several enrollment options are available for individuals whose educational needs can be met by experiences that do not lead to a university degree. Participants desiring to earn academic credit but not a degree could be enrolled as *special students* and *nondegree students*.

Special Student. The special student category includes undergraduates who may be guest matriculants; workshop participants; conditional enrollees; unclassified, off-campus, nonadmitted students who complete term-by-term applications for credit courses; and enrollees in special programs. Participants pay standard fees and receive credit that does not lead to a Michigan State University degree. Records of participation and performance are kept.

Modification of Existing Procedures

Nondegree Student. The graduate-level student who desires to undertake course work beyond the bachelor's degree but not aimed at a graduate degree may apply for admission to nondegree status. Nondegree status may also be used as a conditional category for students who do not yet qualify for admission to the regular graduate programs. Credit is awarded and may be applied toward a degree after admission to a graduate program. (For the master's degree, the final 30 credits must be earned in a status other than nondegree. For the doctoral degree, credits earned in the nondegree status will be reviewed by the appropriate department or guidance committee to determine acceptability.) Standard fees are assessed. Records of participation and performance are kept.

Participants desiring to enroll in credit courses but not earn credit could be enrolled as *visitors* and *auditors*.

Visitor. Visitor status allows individuals admitted to academic programs to enroll in credit courses on a noncredit basis. Records of participation and performance are kept, but no grade except V is awarded. Standard fees are assessed.

Auditor. Persons who have not been admitted to the University can enroll in credit courses as auditors. They receive no credit for these courses. Standard fees are assessed. The course instructor and chairman of the appropriate department approve applicants according to space availability within sections. No evaluation of performance is made for auditors, although enrollment records are kept.

Participants in special educational activities which offer no credit could be enrolled as *noncredit students*. Noncredit students may participate in a wide range of conferences, institutes, special courses, and workshops which are designed to address specific learning needs. Enrollees receive no credit. Records of participation are kept, but performance of participants is neither evaluated nor recorded. Fees vary according to the nature of individual programs.

The enrollment alternatives outlined above provide sufficient flexibility to accommodate the needs of a wide variety of potential participants. The Task Force suggests no additional enrollment options at this time.

10. The university should publicize the availability of all enrollment options to inform potential participants of varying approaches to meeting educational needs.

11. The university should also investigate the feasibility of providing all participants in noncredit, nondegree educational experiences with appropriate documentation of their participation.

Support Services

The primary functions of the university are the creation and dissemination of knowledge. Experience in the educational enterprise has demonstrated, however, that a variety of ancillary services must undergird the academic function. Students should be admitted with a reasonable expectation of successful participation, an expectation that may be dependent upon personal, administrative, and financial support services.

12. The following minimum support services should be extended to nonconventional participants in university programs: (a) An information and assistance center, possessing public-oriented staff personnel to provide aid and information regarding university resources, services, programs, policies, facilities, etc. Wherever appropriate, the information and assistance center specialists should act as ombudsmen, working to facilitate educational participation and minimize bureaucratic inconvenience. Study, recreational, and parking facilities should be components of the center. (b) Academic advising and appropriate personal counseling services. (c) Appropriate financial aid. Although there are no age restrictions on scholarships, loans, etc., students carrying less than seven credits are ineligible for such awards. Because of work schedules and family responsibilities, nonconventional participants will often carry a credit load below this level. Such students should receive equivalent consideration for financial aid, commensurate with their degree of need and extent of educational participation.

The university's responsibility for providing supportive service is becoming an increasingly controversial issue. Present services, established over many years, absorb a significant part of the university's operating budget. The size and diversity of new audiences, the circumstances under which they participate, and the rising costs of support activities call for the development of criteria by which the university can assess its role and responsibility.

13. As increasingly heterogeneous nonconventional audiences become large parts of the university constituency, the board of trustees should examine the needs of these audiences to determine the university's obligation and capacity to provide appropriate support services.

Credit for Past Experiences

Increased access to university resources will involve participation by numbers of people who have not been enrolled in formal educational programs for some time. Others may never have attended a college or university. All will bring varying and often invaluable experiences with them, experiences which should not be discounted.

The university should not require anyone to enroll in a course whose content he has already mastered through formal study, informal study, or other means.

14. The university should continue and expand the availability of waiver examinations and credit by examination.

15. The university should develop new procedures to evaluate and give academic credit for competence gained through previous life experience or academic background.

Examples of possible innovations include the College Level

75

Examination Program and the Bachelor of Business Administration program now being put into operation by the Board of Regents of the State University of New York. Michigan State University should investigate existing practices and devise innovations directed toward specific fields of knowledge.

Certification

In a credential-conscious society, certification serves several purposes. Advancement or increased compensation may accrue in the occupation of the individual who can document a successfully completed educational experience. Certification also provides a means for verifying certain levels of competence or skill. Additionally, the certificate acts as a symbol of achievement for the individual himself, providing a tangible representation of meaningful accomplishment.

Baccalaureate and graduate degrees are but one type of certificate. Associate of Arts degrees and Educational Specialist degrees offer alternative approaches to documenting educational programs. In addition, the Continuing Education Service, the Cooperative Extension Service, and other units now award certain kinds of specialized certificates, such as those presented to participants in professional seminars. The diverse types of educational programs that constitute lifelong education will require these and other alternative approaches to certification.

16. The university should study and, wherever appropriate, expand or otherwise modify certification alternatives for participants in degree and nondegree lifelong educational programs.

IO

Modification of
Existing Programs

A vast number of current University programs will be of interest to the non-conventional student. Some of these programs will continue unchanged. Others, however, may require modification in order to serve more effectively the broadened scope of needs of the individuals who will be participating in them.

Formal educational experiences usually decline drastically upon completion of a degree or termination of matriculated status. Further, participants often do not have the attitudes necessary for systematic self-initiated learning. Yet more than ever before, individual and social needs call for an ongoing, lifelong involvement in educational activities. Institutions of higher learning have the responsibility to orient audiences to lifelong education and to assist them in building the necessary skills.

17. A fundamental responsibility of the university should be to help students become self-initiating learners. Appropriate course and program objectives should reflect this responsibility.

18. To facilitate recommendation 17, the Learning Service should prepare materials (including media presentations) for distribution to the faculty. These materials should include instructional alternatives and methods of evaluation that emphasize the importance of self-learning. Guidelines for the evaluation of the suitability of the instructional alternatives themselves should be provided.

19. The university should institute an informational program to acquaint citizens of the state of Michigan with the concept of lifelong education, its implications, and existing and emerging opportunities for lifelong learning experiences.

Educational Technology

The size and diversity of groups of learners, the circumstances under which they participate in instructional experiences, and the limitation on economic and manpower resources require the widespread use of technological delivery systems.

New methods and techniques with potential educational relevance are appearing continuously. The Carnegie Commission has estimated that about 10 to 20 percent of all on-campus instruction will be *mediated* (available through electronic or other nonpersonal media rather than through personal contact) by the year 2000. In actuality, this estimate may be much too low. Last year at Michigan State University, for example, about 10 percent of all freshman and sophomore credit hours were mediated by the closed circuit television system alone. Since the 10 percent figure does not include other electronic means, such as audio and video cassette playback machines, digital computers, motion pictures, and the like, the Carnegie Commission estimate seems conservative.

These technological implements hold great promise for facilitating off-campus lifelong education, especially external degrees and semi-independent study. Within a few years a great deal of off-campus lifelong education may be made available through media channels. The Carnegie Commission agrees with this prediction, suggesting that technological mediation will carry much greater amounts of off-campus instruction by the 1980s, increasing perhaps 80 percent or more.

Although Michigan State University leads the world in its on-campus employment of closed circuit television, instructional development, and technology, electronic mediation has had limited use in reaching off-campus students.

20. The university should employ mass media and technology to extend formal educational opportunities to off-campus populations. The number and variety of educational programs available through the mass media should be increased.

Although the academic units should bear primary responsibility for the implementation of this recommendation, they will obviously need to seek the assistance of appropriate organizations and experts on campus, particularly WKAR-TV, WKAR-FM, and WKAR (radio) and the Instructional Media Center. Channels for securing audience response should be developed and used wherever possible.

21. To increase efficiency and effectiveness, the university should centralize the administration of telecommunications services.

This centralization should be a phased process guided by the appropriate central administrative office. Academic and other units should retain production facilities commensurate with their special needs and capacities.

Mass media services for the university, primarily radio and

television broadcast facilities, should be complemented by other existing and emerging technological delivery systems.

22. The university should encourage the use of diverse types of technological delivery systems, such as tapes, cassettes, closed circuit television, cable television, computer-assisted instruction, etc., for all appropriate aspects of lifelong education.

The application of technology to the education of campus-based students as well as to off-campus participants may create a number of major problems. First, standard operating budgets do not provide sufficient funds for the purchase of high-cost instructional materials produced externally. Yet the typical American child devotes twenty-two hours a week to television. Thus, today's university student has been acclimated to media communication styles almost from the moment of his birth. He is accustomed to learning through a wide range of formats. In the future, the university will need to devise operational budgets in which funds are categorized for the purchase of videotapes, audiotapes, motion picture films, computer programs, and similar educational materials.

23. The university should examine its instructional budgets in relation to the potential of multimedia instructional systems for meeting the needs and expectations of new generations of students.

Another major problem arising from the application of technology concerns the creation of original programs. The development of suitable programs for public distribution is an extremely difficult, technical, and expensive undertaking. A single episode of the children's show "Sesame Street," for example, costs over thirty thousand dollars to produce. Programs of this kind are inevitably team efforts. Furthermore, programs of the sort suggested in the recommendations expose the entire university to mass audiences. The university's image and future will be strongly influenced by audience reactions to its productions.

Modification of Existing Programs

24. Michigan State University should expand its present involvement in creating and packaging mediated programs for lifelong education. However, it is critical for the university to limit offerings to programs of the highest quality and, at least initially, wide audience appeal.

In addition, the Educational Policies Committee should examine many academic issues raised by the greatly expanded use of technology. For example: What controls should be exercised over programs transmitted by mass media? Are program review procedures needed? If so, what procedures are appropriate? Should faculty receive extra compensation when they appear in prominent roles on programs distributed over mass media?

A third issue arising from the use of technology concerns the marketing of programs created by the university and its faculty. Through the Educational Development Program, the Instructional Media Center, and closed circuit television, the university has developed a wide variety of high-quality instructional materials over the past ten years. Some of these materials are now being marketed nationally.

25. The university should establish a capability for media publication, distribution, and marketing.

In a short period of time, such an operation would probably become not only self-supporting but would also contribute to the financial backing for the development of new and improved educational products.

Although reliance on educational technology may be perfectly suitable to many participants and for many learning experiences, some people may require a more supervised setting. Individuals who have not participated in education for some years might need the support offered by personal contact. Others will find technologically facilitated study too solitary to be rewarding. In any event, all participants should have the opportunity to benefit from the interaction possible through face-to-face contact with faculty members.

26. Programs mediated through technological delivery systems should offer an appropriate amount of contact with teaching faculty and fellow participants.

The "appropriate amount" will be determined by subject matter, predisposition and progress of participants, and evaluative and certifying requirements. In some instances this contact may entail either standard or abbreviated periods of residence on campus.

Degree Programs

At the bachelor's level, Michigan State University grants the degrees of Bachelor of Arts, Bachelor of Fine Arts, Bachelor of Science, Bachelor of Landscape Architecture, and Bachelor of Music. All of these programs require that at least forty credits be earned on the East Lansing campus after reaching junior status.

At the master's level, the university offers the degrees of Master of Arts, Master of Arts for Teachers, Master of Business Administration, Master of Fine Arts, Master of Labor and Industrial Relations, Master of Landscape Architecture, Master of Music, Master of Science, Master of Social Work, and Master in Urban Planning. Usually a minimum of thirteen credits toward the master's degree must be earned on campus, although the Colleges of Education, Business, and Engineering offer off-campus degrees in selected locations.

Residence requirements exclude individuals whose work or family responsibilities prevent attendance of campus classes. Although degree programs might extend personal enrichment or occupational advancement, such people are effectively denied these benefits.

27. The university should review and amend its residence requirements to permit the extension of appropriate degrees to audiences who cannot attend campus classes.

28. The colleges of Michigan State University should offer baccalaureate degree programs appropriate to the interest of off-campus audiences and develop means for making those programs available.

29. Current programs of off-campus study leading to graduate degrees at the master's level should be continued. Colleges should identify other appropriate master's degree programs of interest to off-campus students and develop means for making these programs available.

The Task Force on Lifelong Education does not recommend that Michigan State University offer external degree programs beyond the master's level at this time.

Nondegree Programs

Nondegree formats range from auditing regular courses and enrollment in the evening college (under the Continuing Education Service) through seminars, conferences, and short courses, to the individually based problem-solving characteristic of cooperative extension. The learning experience not oriented to a degree is potentially the most effective answer to many lifelong educational needs.

30. In establishing credit programs that are not degree-oriented, the academic units of the university should give priority to development of programs aimed at: (a) the educationally neglected* and economically distressed; (b) professionals seeking skill updating and improvement; and (c) those who need certification for completion of a program for job change or advancement.

For noncredit programs, all university units, academic as well as service, should assign significant priority to programs serving: (a) the educationally neglected and economically

---

* The term *educationally neglected* refers to those persons heretofore inadequately served by institutions of higher learning. The educationally neglected consist of the disadvantaged, the elderly, minorities, the occupationally displaced, women, and the socially distressed.

distressed; (b) individuals seeking skill updating and improvement; and (c) educational and social institutions attempting to develop independent educational capacities.

The Bachelor of General Studies

To balance recent emphasis on career-oriented education, the university should provide variety and flexibility in learning opportunities that address the unique needs of participants seeking a less specialized, more general course of study. These participants include employed people who need a college degree for advancement or increased compensation; young people who want to adapt to the increasing amount of lateral vocational mobility in early work years by preparing themselves for a variety of possible jobs; people who wish to complete a degree as a meaningful way of employing leisure time; and people who desire a curriculum grounded in a broad interdisciplinary experience of the arts, humanities, and sciences.

An estimated 25 percent of the population of Michigan lives within seventy miles of the Michigan State University campus.* In Lansing alone, as many as six thousand civil service employees are locked into present job classifications because they lack college degrees (estimate prepared under the direction of the Michigan Civil Service Commission Board). University College can identify several hundred mature adults at freshman and sophomore levels (and there may be many more proportionately at upper division levels) who need access to a degree program scheduled at night, on weekends, and in nonconventional formats.

These individuals have unique backgrounds, often having transferable credits from three or more institutions. They do not need restrictive majors; they need complementary courses and courses to fill the gaps in programs previously begun. They are highly motivated and have purposes that do not fit neatly into major

* Michigan State University College of Education, "Friendly Amendments: The College of Education Response to the Preliminary Report of the Task Force on Lifelong Education," January 1973, p. 11.

programs designed for students who enroll immediately after secondary school.

Programs aimed at fulfilling the needs of these individuals are operating in several institutions across the United States. Usually they are labeled general studies or individual studies degrees. Although different in detail, they share two features. First, they use an interdisciplinary or multidisciplinary approach and avoid narrow or restrictive specialization. Second, course requirements are categorized on an individual basis. The participant and his adviser shape a course of study according to personal requirements and preferences.

31. The university, employing all appropriate academic resources, should design and offer a Bachelor of General Studies for both campus and off-campus students.

The extent of identified educational needs that might be successfully met by a Bachelor of General Studies degree renders an immediate response imperative. Several colleges are possible sponsors of such a degree—the College of Arts and Letters, the College of Communication Arts, the College of Natural Science, the College of Social Science, University College, and the College of Urban Development. An initial development of a general studies degree within one unit, however, should not preclude the offering of individualized degrees by other units.

The university should be careful to prevent duplication of effort. In a state possessing twenty-nine community colleges, many of which offer two-year liberal studies curricula, the university should take care to avoid infringing upon the functions of other institutions.

32. Michigan State University should offer any Bachelor of General Studies degree predominantly at the upper division (junior-senior) level.

II

New
Programs

$\mathbf{M}$any individuals who
spoke with the Task Force questioned the wisdom of expanding the
involvement of Michigan State University in lifelong education.
Especially in regard to new programs, they cited formidable obsta-
cles. Quantitative market data is scarce and ambiguous. Budgeting
and organizational conflicts might arise between present university
activities and many new kinds of lifelong educational programs.
Perhaps most important, an expansion of involvement will inevitably
cost money in a period wherein severe financial constraints are imposed already upon most colleges and universities.

Repeatedly, the Task Force was heartened by a fact that
surfaced very early in its deliberations. Michigan State University
is, in fact, already a lifelong university. In discussing ideas initially
thought to be speculative, the Task Force often found that these

ideas were being implemented in programs and activities. This is indicated in the recommendations by the frequency of words such as *expand* and *increase* rather than *begin* or *create*.

Even so, to meet current and emerging needs for lifelong education, new programs inevitably will be required. Could the Task Force design such new programs? Their designs and administration would be dependent upon, among other things, the kinds of learners for whom the program is intended, the geographical locations in which the program is offered, the needs which the program addresses, and the subject matter it includes.

The Task Force did not attempt to identify these factors or to outline in detail any variety of actual programs for three reasons. First, such specificity would have demanded expertise and resources that the task force members did not possess, as well as an investigation substantially different from the sort they contemplated. Second, the Task Force felt that it would be inappropriate to assume responsibility for decisions more appropriately made by the academic units. The colleges and departments, as entities most aware of their own resources and most familiar with the state of their respective disciplines, are well suited to cooperate with both campus and community audiences in establishing program objectives and content. In an integrated system, the primary responsibility for initiative and involvement in lifelong education properly remains with the academic units. Finally and most important, learners served, locations, course content, and objectives are all influenced by constantly changing social conditions. Thus, recommendations dealing with program design had to focus on *process* rather than on details that might be rendered outmoded by changing circumstances. The following section outlines a project for initiating that process.

Learning occurs continuously within individuals and communities whether or not any educational institution is involved. The institution, however, can offer many resources to improve the reliability and efficiency of the process. If the university is to interact with more and different citizens throughout their adult lives, it must do so by taking account of the needs and interests of the citizens, as one of many social and educational institutions contributing

87

directly or indirectly to individual and group learning. The task force assumes: *(1) A wide variety of groups in the society can and will make a useful contribution to the delivery of expanded services. To the extent possible, the university will seek to involve resource people from the community in educational programs.*

Greater access and new kinds of learning experiences must be provided, principally at the local level. The new patterns of interaction explicit in the recommendations of the Task Force will require an ongoing assessment of many aspects of community life, including groups and their educational needs, present and potential problems that need to be researched, available learning resources, channels for the dissemination and use of knowledge, and ways in which the university may combine its efforts in effective and complementary relationships with other agencies and institutions. Useful and reliable programing may depend upon cooperation and the flow of information among the academic units of various educational organizations and their target localities throughout the state. To bring about such cooperation and communication, the university must expand its existing linkages into a community lifelong education system.

Recognizing the variation in needs and priorities of different communities, it is both inappropriate and impossible to predetermine the shape of a lifelong educational program in any given locale. Thus, a community lifelong educational system would be most valuable if established in response to experience, shaped by and to a degree shaping the conditions under which it operates. It should be an evolving system based upon the currently existing network of relationships.

Despite the extensive lessons taught by past involvements and the activities of other universities, there are many unanswered questions about lifelong education and its place in the community. The assumptions of the Task Force provide only broad and provisional answers to such questions. Since Michigan State University must venture into an expanded program of lifelong education against a backdrop of severe fiscal constraint, the testing and refinement of these assumptions should precede the full implementation of many recommendations.

The Task Force, therefore, seeks a mechanism for the *ongoing* assessment of local, regional, and statewide conditions affecting lifelong education. The mechanism attempts to ensure that academic units are armed with accurate and appropriate data before actually entering into programing of a given sort in a given area. This, in turn, should guarantee timely and effective educational experiences.

> *33. Michigan State University should establish an experimental Community Lifelong Education Project. The project should encompass one or more communities and work with them to: (a) define appropriate lifelong education needs, techniques, and target populations; (b) explore interinstitutional linkages for providing lifelong education at the local level; (c) examine organizational patterns for relating the university to the community; and (d) evaluate costs and benefits associated with various program alternatives.*

> *34. The community or communities chosen for the Community Lifelong Education Project should be committed to the project and give evidence of this commitment. They should be large enough to allow the university to explore a full range of interrelated problems and at the same time small enough for the project to have a measurable impact. Finally, each community selected should have existing university offices or programs.*

Because of the complexity of any process that attempts to develop new relationships or functions, the implementation of this recommendation must be phased so as not to preclude full participation by individuals and institutions representing varying constituencies within the community. Nonetheless, any phased implementation must recognize the need for overlap and continuity of established functions.

The initial responsibilities to be fulfilled by the project should include identifying and establishing cooperative relationships with existing university programs and facilities within specified regions; establishing relationships with other educational institutions, community leaders, and decision makers; and participating in the identification of major areas of interest or concern in the communities.

The second stage of implementation should include a comprehensive assessment of the community, including the collection of existing data in major areas, the identification of specific audiences, the exploration of possible alternatives and objectives, and the determination of priorities. This stage may require the involvement of university-based staff support.

Upon completion of the second stage, the Community Lifelong Education Project should be staffed by three to five people in each selected locale. Each staff member should have expertise in a field in which there is much public interest, such as medicine, criminal justice, education, or municipal government. Placed in designated areas for an initial period of three to five years, this staff would not be expected only to study or do research of a theoretical or abstract nature. Their functions should also include assisting other organizations and agencies to conduct their own lifelong educational programs; acting as a bridging or facilitating link between the community and the academic units of the university; consulting activities by on-site personnel for specific problem-solving; evaluating and refining lifelong educational programs; and collaborating with community leaders and constituents in developing suitable and effective programs to meet educational needs.

The university should view the Community Lifelong Education Project not as an end in itself but as a vehicle for broadening understanding to lifelong learning and testing new concepts, procedures, and organizational structures. The project should thus enable the university to assess a wide range of proposals for lifelong education. A second important feature of the community lifelong education project should be the provision of a mechanism capable of evaluating project performance. The mechanism should provide for personnel whose sole responsibility is the evaluation of results of alternative programs.

New Programs

35. A major responsibility of the Community Lifelong Education Project should be to determine the relevance of its activities to communities throughout the state and to recommend to the university and other social and educational institutions procedures for implementing effective programs.

36. Before establishing a Community Lifelong Education Project, the university should carefully define program objectives to provide a basis for designing and evaluating an optimal project.

37. The Community Lifelong Education Project should include a group of professionals whose responsibility is to assist the local staff in studying and evaluating the ongoing effectiveness of lifelong educational programs in participating communities.

At this time it is difficult to predict what new organizational structures, operational procedures, and programs will emerge from the development of the proposed project. Regional programs may become extensive. Local advisory councils, composed of community leaders and their constituents, may be established to assist in planning, coordinating, and evaluating programs.

In the meantime, the university should continue its present efforts to increase the effectiveness of existing community-based programs.

38. To increase the efficiency and effectiveness of Michigan State University's operations within municipalities, counties, or other specified regions, the various off-campus units should, wherever feasible, pool physical and academic support services, share research and applied data, and integrate and coordinate educational programs.

As outlined, the Community Lifelong Educational Project involves a large expenditure of manpower and financial resources. The university is unable to absorb such costs with its current operational budget.

39. The university should seek external funding from appropriate private or government sources to finance the first five years of the community lifelong education project.

Since such sources are more receptive to providing development funds than to supporting ongoing programs, the project should attempt to design and offer services and learning experiences eligible for eventual state subsidization.

12

Organizational Arrangements: Majority View

Lifelong educational activities at American land grant institutions have traditionally been conducted through extension units or departments classified as agricultural (mainly the Cooperative Extension Service) or nonagricultural, general extension structures. Nationally, organizational relationships between agricultural and general extension units fall into four broad patterns: (1) Cooperative extension and general extension have no administrative relationships. (2) Cooperative extension and general extension are headed by different people, both of whom report to the chief extension officer of the institution. (3) Cooperative extension and general extension have been merged into a single admin-

93

istrative unit directed by the chief extension officer of the institution. (4) Cooperative extension has its own staff and resources, while the separate academic units of the institutions carry out general extension activities. All units report to the chief academic officer of the institution.

The organizational patterns of the Cooperative Extension Service and general extension units have been undergoing study and modification over the last two decades. A 1970 survey of the National Association of State Universities and Land-Grant Colleges' Council on Extension employed the categories outlined above to classify its membership. Of ninety-two institutions, seventy-six responded to the questionnaire. Of these, twenty-nine indicated that they had no cooperative extension service, while the remaining forty-seven were distributed as follows into each of the four patterns: twenty-nine institutions followed the first pattern; five institutions followed the second pattern; eleven institutions followed the third pattern; and two institutions followed the fourth pattern. This information led the task force to an assumption: *(m) A variety of of models for offering lifelong education are currently available, some of which are more appropriate for Michigan State University than others.*

At Michigan State University, the Cooperative Extension Service is located within the College of Agriculture and Natural Resources, largely employing its own staff and resource faculty from six other colleges. The director of the Cooperative Extension Service reports through the dean of the college to the provost, who, in turn, reports directly to the university president and the board of trustees.

The Continuing Education Service provides centralized administrative services for the various academic units of the university. Although there are Full-Time Equivalent (FTE) positions budgeted within a number of colleges for continuing educational activities, these account for a minority of the actual programs available. The remainder are conducted by departmental faculty who are compensated on an overload schedule from the budget of the Continuing Education Service. The director of continuing education, like the academic deans, reports directly to the provost.

Organizational Arrangements: Majority View

Cooperative Extension and the Continuing Education Service constitute most, though not all, of the university involvement in lifelong education. In the light of a desire to expand that involvement, the task force felt that any new organizational structure must provide for the performance of eight functions: (1) monitoring and coordinating lifelong educational opportunities, with budgetary responsibility; (2) stimulating or catalyzing innovative opportunities in lifelong education; (3) evaluating lifelong educational programs; (4) establishing community liaison, as a contact point which is visible and oriented toward public needs in lifelong education; (5) overseeing centralized managerial services for the facilitation of lifelong educational activities; (6) continuing cooperation with other agencies and institutions in the interest of effective and efficient lifelong educational opportunities at both state and community levels; (7) soliciting funds from private and governmental sources for lifelong educational projects and programs; and (8) providing overall policy direction for an integrated and coordinated system of university lifelong educational functions in response to demonstrated needs.

Prior to recommending an organizational arrangement to accomplish these functions, the Task Force studied three alternatives: (1) An autonomous unit that would possess centralized administrative authority and its own faculty and instructional resources and would operate independently of the other academic units of the university. The Cooperative Extension Service and the general extension programs offered by the institution would all be subsumed within this unit. (2) An expansion of the role of the provost to include accountability for increased quantity and quality of lifelong educational opportunities. Additional staff to maintain this responsibility would be added to the office of the provost. The Cooperative Extension Service and other lifelong educational programs would report through their respective deans to the provost. (3) A vice-president for lifelong education, regarding whom two possibilities were envisioned. The first possibility involves the vice-president maintaining a staff relationship to the president while empowered with budgetary authority for managerial services necessary to facilitate lifelong education. He would cooperate with the office of the provost, which would retain budgetary responsibility for all academic programs. The second possibility involves the vice-president maintaining budgetary responsibility and position control for lifelong educational activities based in the academic units, including Cooperative Extension. The Cooperative Extension Service and other lifelong educational programs would report to the vice-president through the deans of the respective colleges.

The alternatives were discussed according to the likelihood that they would, among other things: elevate lifelong education to the status of a primary function of the institution; provide a highly visible and prestigious access point to enhance communication between participating faculty members and the community; facilitate coordination and cooperation between the Cooperative Extension Service and other lifelong education programs; increase the involvement of faculty members with expertise in individual lifelong education projects; increase the likelihood that lifelong education responsibilities would be assumed as standard or "part of load" among a large proportion of faculty members; place lifelong education within the sphere of central administrative policy-making bodies, including the board of trustees; and enable the university to adapt continuously to changing social needs for lifelong education.

At Michigan State University, the concept of an autonomous unit has potential limitations. Its separate faculty and programs might lead to an unacceptable degree of conflict and duplication. It is expensive and prohibitively so in times of fiscal restraint. Most important, however, an autonomous unit can seldom draw on the entire resources of the university. The segregation of lifelong education faculty and programs within a separate system might deny many audiences access to the programs and personnel best suited to serve them, or it might lead to an academic hierarchy or class system on the basis of the perceived educational priorities of the institution.

Again within the context of Michigan State University, a vice-presidency, while not necessarily preventing an integrated response, could lead to a sharpening of functional distinctions between lifelong education and other academic programs. A vice-presidency

96

would also necessitate the establishment of a complicated and duplicative reporting procedure between itself and the academic units, forcing them to serve, in effect, two masters. In addition to interposing a new layer of bureaucracy, a vice-presidency might become embroiled in serious budgetary competition with the office of the provost and with other units.

If it is desirable for the academic units to bear primary responsibility for initiating and conducting lifelong education activities, the central administration of lifelong education should be carried out by the chief academic officer of the institution. (Administering lifelong education through an existing office should also lessen time and expenses for starting new programs.)

At Michigan State University, the chief academic administrator is the provost. Although many of the duties necessary to facilitate lifelong education are currently performed by the office of the provost, the elevation of lifelong education as an institutional priority would require an intensification of effort. An efficient and effective integration of lifelong education necessitates the involvement of an administrator with both staff and budget. The duties of the provost are already extensive, however, and present organizational arrangements delegate primarily staff responsibilities to the assistant provosts.

40. A reorganization of the Office of the Provost should be undertaken, directed by the president and assisted by the provost and other appropriate personnel, in order for that office to more effectively administer lifelong education. This organization should enhance the role of the provost's office in coordination and innovation.

41. For the present, the Cooperative Extension Service should continue to report through the dean of the College of Agriculture and Natural Resources. However, the Office of the Provost should periodically review the relationships between the Cooperative Extension Service, the Continuing Education Service, and other lifelong educational programs to ensure the effectiveness and suitability of organizational arrangements.

42. A permanent advisory committee should be established to assist the Office of the Provost in coordinating lifelong educational programs and activities, including those offered by the Cooperative Extension Service and other units of the institution.

Upon completion of the recommended reorganization, the office of the provost should assume responsibility for lifelong education at Michigan State University. Its duties should include: (1) monitoring, coordinating, and evaluating lifelong education programs in relation to evolving individual and community needs; (2) stimulating new lifelong education opportunities and projects; (3) overseeing the phased centralization of the university telecommunications system, and effectively relating that system to others developed in the state; (4) administering the Kellogg Center and the regional continuing education centers, conference and institute program, and telecommunications system of the university; (5) engaging in community-university liaison, enunciating the mission of lifelong education, and providing visible access points, information, and assistance to the public, faculty, staff, and student body; (6) providing required managerial and facilitating services in support of lifelong education activities; (7) maintaining cooperative relationships with external agencies and institutions and, where appropriate, developing collaborative arrangements in the interest of effective and efficient lifelong education programs at both state and community levels; (8) developing budgets and obtaining funds for lifelong education programs and support services and seeking resources from private foundations and federal and state governments to support lifelong education; (9) providing direction and management for the community lifelong education project; and (10) maintaining, both on and off campus, a total university response capability for relating institutional resources to complex educational problems of interdisciplinary character.

The Task Force assumes that in the reorganization of the office of the provost several subunits currently administered by the Continuing Education Service will be examined. These subunits include the Highway Traffic Safety Center, the Institute for Community Development, the Pewabic Pottery Center, and the Abrams Planetarium.

43. Except for the Kellogg Center and the regional continuing education centers, conference and institute program, and telecommunications system of the university, all units within the Continuing Education Service should be reviewed to determine whether they might be more appropriately housed in one of the academic units of the university or within the Office of the Provost.

Appointing an assistant dean or coordinator for continuing education in each of the academic colleges of the university has proven effective and valuable. Changed conditions and responsibilities may or may not require new administrative arrangements.

44. Deans should examine administrative arrangements within their respective colleges to determine their suitability for facilitating an expanded involvement in lifelong education.

13

Organizational Arrangements: Minority View

The Task Force is divided on the issue of locus and role of the principal administrator for lifelong education. On two occasions tie votes were cast. Action by the chair resolved the tie votes; it did not resolve the dilemma posed by the issue. The basic recommendation in the report is that general administrative responsibility for lifelong education should be lodged in a reorganized office of the provost. Ten of the members of the Task Force respectfully dissent from that recommendation and present a rationale for both their dissent and their alternative recommendation.

Organizational Arrangements: Minority View

The ten dissenting members cannot accept the basic premise that lifelong education is (simply) an academic function and should be administered as such by the chief academic officer. Neither can they accept the arguments and recommendation built upon this premise. They see lifelong education as involving several major functions, only some of which are essentially academic. These members feel that the resolution of policy and strategy issues posed by the recommended new thrust in lifelong education should involve but not be confined to internal academic structures and traditional academic modes for making and implementing decisions.

Lifelong education includes a set of complex components, most of which have great implications for the university. Some are unique and require special administrative provisions. Others represent extensions of work appropriately administered within the office of the provost or other units. Such units, in their lifelong education contributions, should be coordinated within an integrated system but not subordinated to an additional level of bureaucracy.

In view of these realities and in order to give emphasis and visibility to lifelong education, assure access to the president and executive group, centralize administrative and coordinative responsibility, reduce red tape and conflicts of interest, and enhance prompt and university-level response to needs and issues as they arise, the ten dissenting members of the Task Force strongly believe that the general administrative responsibility for lifelong education at Michigan State University should be vested in a chancellor or vice-president.

They see six major components (described in the following paragraphs) in the comprehensive program of lifelong education that the Task Force proposed. Only one, though assuredly the major one, is necessarily lodged in the office of the provost, but lifelong education would not prosper if all of the components were administered within that office.

The *academic component,* instruction and research, constitutes the sine qua non of lifelong education. The office of the provost and the vice-president for research development should assume responsibility for it. Each college, as it develops an integrated effort in

101

lifelong education, should be funded for it through regular program budgeting processes of the appropriate office. Principal responsibility for program quality and renewal should lie with the academic units. The vice-president should monitor programs, however, and consult on budget allocations. To assist innovation, to start programs, or to supply specially needed short-term contributions in lifelong education, the vice-president should have adequate funds.

The *student service component* includes counseling, financial assistance, and other services important to lifelong education. Special competence and resources should be provided, as are academic services, by the university unit best equipped to provide them. The vice-president for lifelong education should be supportive in interpreting needs and providing funds for these services.

A *complex communication and technology component* presently includes radio, television (broadcast, cable, and closed circuit), computer and publication units, and their ties into a variety of networks. These represent the beginnings of a system; its expansion has enormous implications for the entire university. If evolving technology produces, as predicted by the Carnegie Commission (1972a, p. 2), a change from "the historical requirements-met-through-teaching approach" and makes feasible (p. 94) "the combined capacity of making available to any student, anywhere in the country, at any time, learning from the total range of accumulated human knowledge," the university will be rendered either fundamentally different or obsolete, and the concept of student admission will become virtually meaningless.

The vice-president should have charge of the university telecommunication system and its interrelationships with wider systems. As administrator of this potent set of instruments with their profound implications for virtually every function of the university, he should be closely related to the president and participate directly and regularly in the highest level policy and strategy deliberations.

A *facilities and support services component* is required to serve nonconventional students in nonconventional ways. Some special facilities and services such as residence halls and registration services can be provided by established university units. Others, such as off-campus county and metropolitan offices, the Kellogg Center, and conference management services, are unique and must be specially established and administered. As the volume of lifelong education increases, coordination and management in this area, already a major enterprise, will increase in importance. The function belongs in a special unit under the vice-president for lifelong education.

An *extensive diplomatic component* is needed for an increasingly intricate network of relationships, most of which have highly significant implications for the university. The balance of sovereignty will shift. Increasingly autonomous, diverse, and dispersed students will have firmly held definitions of need and criteria of excellence. A variety of professional and special-interest groups will insist upon involvement in program and policy decisions. The university must accommodate its work in one way or another to community colleges, public and private regional colleges, universities and coalitions, and government agencies at various levels. Communications media, in addition to those which collaborate in instruction, may misinterpret the university's work in communities across the state and beyond. Lifelong education involves community interaction.

The vice-president for lifelong education will have as one of his persistent and important tasks negotiating and monitoring collaborative agreements; maintaining relationships with urban, county, state, and federal governments; eliciting and maintaining cooperation between university personnel, community leaders, and participants in learning experiences; sharing evaluation and planning with bona fide representatives of disparate participant groups; and maintaining an accurate interpretation of the intentions and functions of the university in lifelong education.

This component will be shared with colleges, county and metropolitan offices, individual faculty members, and other university representatives. It is important, however, that the vice-president provide leadership, integrity, and rationality in this essentially diplomatic function. The sensitivity and significance of this work commend it to the closest possible involvement with central university policy and strategy.

Patterns for Lifelong Learning

The *general leadership and advocacy component* recognizes that lifelong education involves a complex and unusual set of operations. It has major implications, both internal and external, for the whole university. Its healthy development depends upon willing contribution and change in many academic and service units. It also depends upon the vision, diplomacy, autonomy, and leadership ability of its general administrative officer and his staff.

That officer and staff must coordinate major contributions administered by others, administer those which are unique to the special thrusts of lifelong education, negotiate a complex network of policy and practice arrangements with external institutions, provide rationale and implement support for needed change, and both personify and proclaim the vision of lifelong education held by the university.

In many universities the dilemma of the lifelong education enterprise is that it cannot be fully subsumed as a component of an academic unit, nor can any academic unit be fully subordinated to lifelong education. Academic units and lifelong education are intensely interdependent and their respective administrative officers can best stand coequal in rank, each supporting and each admonishing the other. Together they serve the total mission of the university under policies and through strategies that each shares in shaping.

We have measured the various major functions to be performed, and the alternative patterns for administering them, against the seven criteria unanimously agreed upon by the Task Force, as stated on page 96. It was the firm conclusion of the ten dissenting Task Force members that the general administrator of lifelong education at Michigan State University should stand immediately adjacent to the president and that he should bear the title chancellor or vice-president or such other title as the president and board of trustees deem appropriate. In academic matters he should function as an associate provost; in other matters and in off-campus relations he should be the vice-president.

I4

Major Academic and Financial Concerns

The university must ensure the integrity of its standards. All of its programs must meet comparable, though not necessarily identical, criteria for the quality of their content and methods. The Task Force assumes that lifelong education will observe the exacting gauge to which Michigan State University has long submitted itself. Goals and expectations should be clearly articulated before beginning any program; accountability, as it relates to quality, depends upon a careful definition of educational ends by both the university and participating audiences.

45. All university lifelong education programs must be of the highest quality in accordance with the objectives of the learning experience they offer.

105

Continuance and expansion of any program should depend upon demonstration of high quality, effectiveness in achieving objectives, and favorable student interest and response.

46. Quality should be continually monitored through procedures developed for the joint evaluation of offerings by program participants and the academic and administrative units which support the program.

Such units will include departments, colleges, academic governance bodies, the office of the provost, and various combinations of these. Responses of participants should be examined during, as well as after, the completion of programs.

47. To determine the extent to which various lifelong education experiences serve long-term needs, time-lapse surveys should be conducted with representative samples of participants.

The resulting data should be considered in the design of new programs as well as the rating of existing ones.

In discussing the response of the faculty to an expansion of lifelong education at Michigan State University, the Task Force relied on the following assumptions: *(n) New clientele and new delivery systems in the university necessitate a philosophic commitment to lifelong education by faculty, staff, and administration and require added teaching skills and changes of methodology. (o) The interests, training, and commitments of many of the present faculty are directed to professional services other than those which are necessary to meet the lifelong educational needs of diverse populations and unique educational settings.*

Until now, little systematic development and evaluation have been devoted to lifelong education. Data are inadequate regarding the unique needs and problems of groups that will constitute new audiences. Few faculty and staff personnel have well-developed specializations in lifelong education.

The university must intensify the process of developing a

talent pool as a source of expertise for the lifelong education program. At the same time, the institution must increase its efforts to orient and inform faculty, staff, students, and public constituents about what lifelong education is, why it is crucially important, and what is being done to implement it.

48. The university should expand its criteria for faculty hiring, embodying in that expansion components that will ensure the employment of a greater percentage of faculty familiar with, concerned about, and capable of lifelong educational activities.

49. Criteria for salary increases, promotions in academic rank, and the awarding of tenure should reflect the lifelong education efforts of faculty members proportionate to other accepted criteria.

50. The university should especially encourage the academic units to provide for travel opportunities and allowances, study sabbaticals, released time for program development, and other mechanisms to encourage faculty members to increase their expertise and involvement in lifelong educational activities.

On its present operational budget, the university is unable to undertake an effort of the scope recommended here. New funds are necessary but are difficult to obtain because of current fiscal limitations at local, state, and national levels. The Task Force recognized these constraints in the following assumptions: *(p) Although a market exists for lifelong educational opportunities, that market is sensitive to costs and convenience. (q) Expanded lifelong education, which is increasingly relevant to present and emerging social reality, requires additional financial resources. (r) Foundations are receptive to financing development costs, experimental programs, and similar activities but are generally unwilling to support continuing operational programs and are also unlikely to maintain a program of lifelong education.* The Task Force, therefore, supports a diversified approach to financing lifelong education.

51. To finance developmental costs and initial operations of experimental lifelong educational projects (e.g., the Community Lifelong Education Project), Michigan State University should seek grants from appropriate foundations.

52. The university should encourage state, county, and municipal governmental units to extend partial or full fiscal support to lifelong educational activities of community benefit.

53. In commercially oriented lifelong educational activities undertaken at the request of corporations or other entities, the university should contract with those entities to absorb programming costs.

54. In problem-oriented lifelong educational activities, the university should seek fiscal support from governmental agencies and departments at the appropriate level (local, state, or federal).

Except for the Cooperative Extension Service and conventional degree programs, lifelong education has generally not been supported by legislative appropriations. Nonetheless, many individuals seeking lifelong educational experiences are already supporting educational institutions through state, federal, and local taxes. Such persons contribute a great share of present subsidies. They should have the opportunity to make use of the university resources underwritten by those subsidies.

55. The university should strongly urge ongoing state support of appropriate lifelong education activities.

Tuition for credit-enrolled students in the 1972–1973 academic year was, for Michigan residents on campus, fifteen and sixteen dollars per credit hour (undergraduate and graduate); for nonresidents on campus, thirty-four and thirty-five dollars per credit hour (undergraduate and graduate); and for both undergraduates and graduates off campus, twenty-three dollars per credit hour. Off-campus tuition has been higher than on-campus tuition because of the state legislature's policy that off-campus activities of Michigan State University should be self-supporting.

Tuition for noncredit enrollees varies according to the nature and cost of individual activities and, in some cases, according to the extent of costs that may be borne by sponsoring groups. After examining the circumstances under which many potential audiences participate in lifelong education, the task force arrived at the following recommendation:

56. Tuition for credit-enrolled participants should be equal both on and off campus.

An expanded role in lifelong education will require appropriate budget mechanisms. Significant budget flexibility must be ensured to encourage constructive experimental and developmental activities. At the same time, funds allocated for ongoing lifelong educational programs must be protected from gradual diversion to other areas.

After examining alternatives, the Task Force chose the educational development program of the university as a viable budget model. The educational development program is a discretionary funding mechanism within the office of the provost. Faculty may apply for grants for innovative projects aimed at improving undergraduate education. Funds are transferred for a limited period of time into the operating budgets of departments or colleges receiving grants.

57. The university should seek financial support to establish a lifelong education grants program. The Office of the Provost should administer the program, allocating funds to support appropriate developmental or experimental projects.

Projects should be eligible for grants if they are: innovative and experimental; directed primarily to nonconventional students; amenable to evaluation and indicative of potential for improving the quality of lifelong education; generalizable—applicable in many regions of the state, appropriate for other units of the university, or relevant to diverse populations of learners; relevant to larger numbers of learners than other projects; and if the understanding is clear that if the project is successful, deans, department chairmen, and involved faculty members will cooperate to seek funds for its continuation.

For the support of their regular and expanding work in lifelong education, academic units must have a budget system that provides flexibility and accountability. In the past, ongoing lifelong education activities have been adjuncts to duties of the academic units. Although budget allotments were once made to several departments for regular lifelong education responsibilities, the practice atrophied because such funds were frequently diverted to other programs and activities. Faculty could be attracted to efforts outside their conventional teaching assignments only by payment on an overload basis. The task force assumed that: *(s) Resources of the university which may be relevant to lifelong education are not now fully used in expanding educational opportunities for the citizens of the state. The university should seek to optimize the use of existing internal resources devoted to lifelong learning. (t) In view of the changing social context, the university may need to reexamine how internal resources are allocated for lifelong education.*

The Task Force on Lifelong Education urges that lifelong education be accepted as part of the standard mission of the academic units. The following recommendations aim at encouraging such acceptance:

58. The Office of the Provost should allocate general funds under its control to the units of the university according to a system of program budgeting, with lifelong education activities as an integral part of that system

59. Whenever possible, lifelong education activities should be assigned to faculty members as part of regularly compensated duties. The definition of such duties should take

110

into account added effort and inconvenience incurred in discharging them (for example, travel between the university and regional centers).

60. Upon implementation of the above recommendations, the academic units and the Office of the Provost should cooperate to minimize the use of overload payment.

15

Interinstitutional
Cooperation

Although the Task Force undertook its mission as a response by a single university, perhaps the most crucial point in the report is that lifelong education must be a cooperative endeavor. Michigan State University cannot provide all of the learning experiences needed by the people of the state. All institutions—corporations, government and civil service units, primary and secondary schools, community colleges, vocational and technical schools, and universities—must seek appropriate places within a statewide lifelong education network. Each institution must respect the capacities and prerogatives of its fellows, implementing complementary programs for the greatest educational service to the widest possible audience.

Interinstitutional Cooperation

Michigan has thirteen state-supported four-or-more-year colleges and universities, twenty-nine state-assisted two-year community colleges, forty-seven church-affiliated and private colleges and universities, and a number of other proprietary schools, special institutes, and institutions of postsecondary educational training. While the state board of education has "general planning and co-ordination" responsibility for higher education in the state, its role is essentially recommendatory, especially in relation to Michigan State University, the University of Michigan, and Wayne State University. The Michigan constitution stipulates that these three institutions will be autonomous, with publicly elected governing boards.

The governor's commission on higher education is charged with addressing three major tasks during 1973 and 1974. They are (1) To define the goals of higher education in Michigan, including such matters as who should be educated and for what purposes, the manpower needs of the state now and in the future, the purposes of graduate and undergraduate institutions, and the role of the university, college, and community college. (2) To determine and recommend procedures and processes for governing and coordinating higher education as it relates to both individual institutions and a system of institutions. (3) To determine the financial implications of meeting state goals of higher education, including recommendations about delegating the responsibility for meeting financial needs among state and national governments, private sources, and students and their families. At this time, however, there is no formal, official, or mandatory state system for interinstitutional coordination.

Several organizations have established voluntary cooperative arrangements. Among them are the Michigan Council of State College Presidents (for the thirteen state-supported colleges and universities), the Michigan Community College Association, and the Association of Independent Colleges and Universities of Michigan.

In February 1959 the Council of State College Presidents approved a plan for a coordinated extension system for Michigan. (See the March 9, 1959 statement of "Policies Adopted for the Michigan Coordinating Council of State College Field Services," available from the Executive Director of the Council of State College Presidents. See also the statement of policies relating to required field office operations, April 3, 1959.) This plan created the Coordinating Council of State College Field Services, now called the Coordinating Council for Continuing Higher Education.

The Coordinating Council is composed of two representatives and two alternates appointed annually from each member institution. Since 1959, this council has actively functioned to implement a voluntary statewide system for coordinating programs and services offered by its member institutions.

From 1971–1972, the thirteen state colleges included in the Coordinating Council provided through their field service and continuing education divisions an estimated thirteen hundred undergraduate credit courses, enrolling two thousand "fiscal year equated" (FYE) students and producing sixty thousand student credit hours; twenty-three hundred graduate credit courses, enrolling five thousand FYE students and producing ninety-seven thousand student credit hours; twenty-two hundred noncredit courses, enrolling twelve hundred FYE students and producing the equivalent of thirty-five thousand student credit hours; one thousand conferences, institutes, and workshops, enrolling 110,000 participants (including seventeen hundred FYE students and producing the equivalent of fifty-three thousand student credit hours); and three thousand correspondence courses, enrolling 290 FYE students and producing eighty-seven hundred student credit hours.

The total number of programs (undergraduate and graduate credit courses, noncredit courses, conferences, institutes, workshops, and correspondence courses) made available to the adult public by the thirteen state colleges and universities in Michigan was approximately ninety-eight hundred, with over ten thousand FYE students and generating about 250,000 student credit hours or their equivalent.

The voluntary coordination of lifelong educational programs by state-supported colleges and universities is extensive, but coordination and cooperation occur elsewhere as well. The community colleges and independent colleges, through their associations and the community service divisions, also make a substantial contribution to

114

cooperative lifelong education. None of these, of course, include the extensive statewide programs of Michigan State University's Cooperative Extension Service, a lifelong educational system in itself.

Thus, while no mandatory system currently coordinates post-secondary lifelong education programs and services, voluntary systems are making a significant effort to provide the necessary resources. Nonetheless, these systems sometimes compete, sometimes duplicate, and sometimes fail to provide the full range of opportunities needed by those who seek lifelong learning.

The Task Force adopted the following assumptions relating to interinstitutional cooperation: *(u) Cooperative arrangements among the major universities for providing lifelong education to the people of the state would be most desirable. An interinstitutional consortium will require a major commitment by the administration, faculty, and staff of the various universities in Michigan. (v) Cooperative relationships between Michigan State University and community colleges offer special opportunities to promote lifelong education.* The Task Force then recommended:

> *61. Since no mandatory system exists at the present time for statewide interinstitutional coordination of public and adult lifelong education programs, Michigan State University should continue to cooperate with the twelve other state colleges and universities in the voluntary system of the coordinating council.*

> *62. Since the thirteen state-supported colleges and universities do not represent all of the higher education opportunities of the State, Michigan State University should also make a strong effort to cooperate with public schools, community colleges, independent colleges and universities, public libraries, and other social and educational institutions to develop a comprehensive and coordinated lifelong education network for the state of Michigan.*

No single institution of higher learning can serve all the

115

educational needs of all people. This limitation has led to specific interinstitutional cooperative agreements, consortia, and joint programs.

Michigan State University currently conducts community-based programs and activities through the seven regional centers of the Continuing Education Service, the eighty county offices of the Cooperative Extension Service, and the medical training program of the colleges of medicine (in association with community hospitals). As noted previously, additional extension programs are employed independently by other academic and service units.

Several of the Continuing Education Service regional centers are administered jointly with one or more of the other state colleges or universities. Some are located on the campuses of state or community colleges. Michigan State University, the University of Michigan, and Western Michigan University have approved plans to develop a common "university center" in Grand Rapids on an experimental consortium basis. Joint courses and program offerings are available at several regional centers. A number of special projects, grants, and contracts are being conducted in cooperation with community colleges and other universities. Studies are underway to determine the feasibility of interinstitutional coordination of external degree programs, while special workshops and teacher-training programs are operating within school districts.

Interinstitutional cooperation is difficult but essential. Demands for flexibility and innovation will increase as open access, new instructional technology, and expanded knowledge reshape higher education.

63. Michigan State University should continue lifelong education activities through the regional centers, county offices, and community institutions now operating. Some modification and change may be necessary, however, to accommodate the development and expansion of educational communications, new instructional technology, and a coordinated statewide system of higher education.

116

Interinstitutional Cooperation

The scope of needs, demands, and problems is of such magnitude that interinstitutional cooperation and joint arrangement are essential to any effective response. The Task Force cannot predict what state commissions and agencies may propose, but it does recognize the need for a statewide commitment by all educational institutions to cooperate and engage jointly in fulfilling their responsibilities.

64. Michigan State University should explore its capacities for lifelong education services, using a systematic, coordinated working relationship with other schools, colleges, and universities of the state (public and private). A planned program should include interinstitutional consortia as well as formal and ad hoc contracts and agreements.

65. Through such a systematic, coordinated working relationship, the university should encourage more extensive interinstitutional use, administration, supervision, and/or facilitation of appropriate programs, physical resources, matriculation procedures, program articulation, transfer of credits, and certification.

Many avenues exist for cooperation between the university and the community colleges of Michigan. Complementary and mutually supportive relationships with these institutions might encompass academic programs, physical facilities, community service activities, and many other factors central to lifelong education.

66. The university should develop the closest possible working relationship with community colleges.

The size of potential audiences and the range of needed programs suggest that an effective activity for the university may lie in assisting other institutions to conduct their own lifelong education programs. Cooperation with such institutions in the expansion of in-service educational opportunities represents a means for the university to optimize its scarce resources through "multiplier" effects.

117

67. Strengthening the lifelong educational capacities of local institutions should be a high priority objective of regional operations of the university.

*

With this discussion of interinstitutional cooperation *Patterns for Lifelong Learning* comes to an end. It is an appropriate note upon which to close. Although Part Three focuses its attention upon one institution, these final pages stress a fact of critical importance— only through a comprehensive and coordinated educational system will any systematic process of lifelong learning become a reality for most Americans. A single college or university can play its part— perhaps a crucial part—but there is a role for all.

Appendix:

Task Force Members

**Membership, Steering Committee of Study
on Continuing Education and the Future**

THEODORE M. HESBURGH, C.S.C.—*chairman, president of the
University of Notre Dame*

THOMAS P. BERGIN—*dean, Center for Continuing Education,
University of Notre Dame*

CYRIL O. HOULE—*professor of education, The University
of Chicago*

PAUL A. MILLER—*president, Rochester Institute of Technology*

D. B. VARNER—*president, University of Nebraska*

CLIFTON R. WHARTON, JR.—*president, Michigan State University*

Membership, Task Force on Continuing Education and Social Responsibility

ELIAS BLAKE, JR.—*chairman and president, Institute for Services to Education*

DAVID G. BROWN—*executive vice-president for academic affairs, Miami University*

JOSEPH PAIGE—*dean of education, Federal City College*

KENNETH D. ROOSE—*educational consultant*

THURMAN J. WHITE—*vice-president for continuing education and public service, University of Oklahoma*

Membership, Task Force on Continuing Education and Public Affairs

JOHN BRADEMAS—*chairman, Congressman from Indiana*

JOHN DIXON—*director, Center for a Voluntary Society*

SAMUEL HALPERIN—*director, educational staff seminar, George Washington University*

JOHN W. MACY, JR.—*president, Council of Better Business Bureaus*

JOHN NAISBITT—*chairman, Urban Research Corporation*

LOIS D. RICE—*vice-president, College Entrance Examination Board*

GLEN L. TAGGART—*president, Utah State University*

Membership of the Task Force on Continuing Education and the University

HOWARD R. NEVILLE—*chairman, executive vice-president for administration, University of Nebraska*

WILLARD L. BOYD—*president, University of Iowa*

JERROLD K. FOOTLICK—*education editor, Newsweek*

MORTON GORDON—*professor of education, University of Michigan*

ROSALIND LORING—*assistant dean of university extension, University of California, Los Angeles*

120

Appendix: Task Force Members

WARREN B. MARTIN—*provost, Sonoma State College*
O. MEREDITH WILSON—*president and director, Center for Advanced Study in the Behavioral Sciences*

Membership of the Task Force on Continuing Education for New Knowledge and the Professions

ALEXANDER M. SCHMIDT—*chairman, commissioner of the Food and Drug Administration, U.S. Department of Health, Education, and Welfare*
CECELIA CONRATH—*associate director for continuing education and manpower, Health Services and Mental Health Administration, U.S. Department of Health, Education and Welfare*
W. PHIL HERRIOTT—*director of education and training, United Airlines*
LLOYD M. MORRISETT—*president, John and Mary Markle Foundation*
JOHN W. REED—*professor of law, University of Michigan*

Membership, Task Force on Lifelong Education, Michigan State University

WILLIAM R. WILKIE—*chairman, assistant to the president*
DAVID ANDERSON—*graduate student in English*
PATRICIA BARNES-MCCONNELL—*assistant professor, Center for Urban Affairs*
TONY BENEVIDES—*director, Cristo Rey Community Center, Lansing; community representative*
ALEX CADE—*professor of education and director, Upward Bound Program*
RICHARD CHAPIN—*director of libraries*
ROBERT DAVIS—*assistant provost*
MILDRED ERICKSON—*associate professor, University College*
MICHAEL HARRISON—*professor of physics, faculty grievance officer*
E. C. HAWKINS—*pastor, Friendship Baptist Church, Lansing; community representative*

121

Patterns for Lifelong Learning

ARMAND HUNTER—*director, Continuing Education Service*

MARK JAEGER—*undergraduate student, mathematics*

RUSSELL KLEIS—*professor of administration and higher education*

DANIEL KRUGER—*associate director and professor, labor and industrial relations*

KULLERVO LOUHI—*dean, College of Business*

GEORGE McINTYRE—*director, Cooperative Extension Service*

MARY E. MISSLITZ—*community representative*

BRUCE J. OSTERINK—*alumnus, class of 1965*

EDWARD ROTHMAN—*alumnus, class of 1921*

LAWRENCE VON TERSH—*dean, College of Engineering*

JAMES VOTRUBA—*graduate student, administration and higher education*

CLARENCE WINDER—*dean, College of Social Science*

Bibliography

This brief bibliography contains a listing of all sources used in the book if they are at all likely to be available to the general reader. Of the other references included, a few deal with the history of higher adult education or descriptions of its practice in colleges and universities, but most are either accounts of present activities or proposals for the future.

ALFORD, H. F. *Continuing Education in Action.* New York: Wiley, 1968.

AMERICAN COUNCIL ON EDUCATION. *Higher Education and the Adult Student.* Washington, D.C., 1972.

ARBOLINO, J. N., AND VALLEY, J. R. "Education: The Institution or the Individual." *Continuing Education,* 1970, 3.

ASHBY, E. *Technology and the Academics.* London: Macmillan, 1959.

ASHBY, E. *Any Person, Any Study: An Essay on Higher Education in the United States.* New York: McGraw-Hill, 1971.

ASSEMBLY ON UNIVERSITY GOALS AND GOVERNANCE. *A First Report.* Boston: American Academy of Arts and Sciences, 1971.

123

Bibliography

ASSOCIATION OF UNIVERSITY EVENING COLLEGES AND THE NATIONAL UNIVERSITY EXTENSION ASSOCIATION. *Programs and Registrations 1970–1971.* Norman, Okla., 1972.

AXFORD, R. W. *Adult Education: The Open Door.* New York: Intext, 1969.

BARZUN, J. *The American University.* New York: Harper and Row, 1968.

BASKIN, S. *Higher Education: Some Newer Developments.* New York: McGraw-Hill, 1965.

BEBOUT, J. E. "University Services to the Urban Community." *American Behavioral Scientist,* Feb. 1963, *16*(3).

BERN, H. A. "Universities Without Campuses." *Educational Leadership,* Jan. 1971, *28.*

BIRKBECK COLLEGE. *The University Education of Mature Students.* Four addresses given at a conference on the adult degree. University of London, July 20–22, 1967.

BIRENBAUM, W. M. *Overlive: Power, Poverty, and the University.* New York: Delacorte Press, 1969.

BURCH, G. *Challenge to the University: An Inquiry into the University's Responsibility for Adult Education.* Chicago: Center for the Study of Liberal Education for Adults, 1961.

BURRELL, J. A. *A History of Adult Education at Columbia University.* New York: Columbia University Press, 1954.

CAPES, M. (Ed.) *Communication or Conflict.* New York: Association Press, 1960.

CARNEGIE COMMISSION ON HIGHER EDUCATION. *The Capitol and the Campus: State Responsibility for Post-secondary Education.* New York: McGraw-Hill, 1971a.

CARNEGIE COMMISSION ON HIGHER EDUCATION. *Less Time, More Options: Education Beyond the High School.* New York: McGraw-Hill, 1971b.

CARNEGIE COMMISSION ON HIGHER EDUCATION. *New Students and New Places: Policies for the Future Growth and Development of American Higher Education.* New York: McGraw-Hill, 1971c.

Bibliography

CARNEGIE COMMISSION ON HIGHER EDUCATION. *The Fourth Revolution: Instructional Technology in Higher Education.* New York: McGraw-Hill, 1972a.

CARNEGIE COMMISSION ON HIGHER EDUCATION. *The More Effective Use of Resources: An Imperative for Higher Education.* New York: McGraw-Hill, 1972b.

CARNEGIE COMMISSION ON HIGHER EDUCATION. *Reform on Campus: Changing Students, Changing Academic Programs.* New York: McGraw-Hill, 1972c.

COMMISSION ON NON-TRADITIONAL STUDY. *Diversity by Design.* San Francisco: Jossey-Bass, 1973.

Convergence (Issue on university extension programs), 1971, *4*(3).

COTTON, W. E. *On Behalf of Adult Education.* Boston: Center for the Study of Liberal Education for Adults, Boston University, 1968.

CROSS, K. P. *Beyond the Open Door.* San Francisco: Jossey-Bass, 1971.

DAVIS, C. (Ed.) *The 1,000 Mile Campus.* Los Angeles: Office of the Chancellor, California State University and Colleges, 1972.

DEPPE, D. A. "The Adult Educator: Marginal Man and Boundary Definer." *Adult Leadership,* October 1969, *18*.

DIEKHOFF, J. S. *The Domain of the Faculty in Our Expanding Colleges.* New York: Harper and Row, 1956.

DRUCKER, P. F. *The Age of Discontinuity.* New York: Harper and Row, 1969.

DUKE, C. "Part-Time Students in England." *Journal of the International Congress of University Adult Education,* April 1968, *7.*

DYER, J. *Ivory Towers in the Market Place: The Evening College in American Education.* Indianapolis: Bobbs-Merrill, 1956.

EDUCATIONAL POLICY RESEARCH CENTER. *Alternative Futures and Educational Policy.* Menlo Park, Calif.: Stanford Research Institute, 1970.

EURICH, A. C. (Ed.) *Campus 1980: The Shape of the Future in American Higher Education.* New York: Dell, 1968.

125

Bibliography

EURICH, N., AND SCHWENKMEYER, B. *Great Britain's Open University: First Chance, Second Chance, or Last Chance?* New York: Academy for Educational Development, 1971.

FARMER, M. L. (Ed.) *Counseling Services for Adults in Higher Education.* Metuchen. N.J.: Scarecrow Press, 1971.

FAURE, E., AND OTHERS. *Learning to Be.* Paris: UNESCO, 1972.

FERRIN, R. I. *A Decade of Change in Free-Access Higher Education.* New York: College Entrance Examination Board, 1971.

FLAUGHER, R. L., MAHONEY, M. J., AND MESSIGN, R. B. *Credit by Examination for College-Level Studies: An Annotated Bibliography.* New York: College Entrance Examination Board, 1967.

FOLGER, J. K., ASTIN, H. S., AND BAYER, A. E. *Human Resources and Higher Education.* New York: Russell Sage Foundation, 1970.

FRASER, W. R. *Residential Education.* Oxford: Pergamon Press, 1968.

FURNISS, W. T. *Higher Education for Everybody? Issues and Implications.* Washington, D.C.: American Council on Education, 1971.

GOULD, S. B. *Today's Academic Condition.* New York: McGraw-Hill, 1970.

GOULD, S. B. AND CROSS, K. P. (Eds.) *Explorations in Non-Traditional Study.* San Francisco: Jossey-Bass, 1972.

HAZEN FOUNDATION. *The Student in Higher Education.* New Haven, Conn.: Hazen Foundation, 1968.

HODGKINSON, H. L. *Institutions in Transition: A Study of Changes in Higher Education.* New York: McGraw-Hill, 1971.

HOPPE, W. A. (Ed.) *Policies and Practices in Evening Colleges, 1971.* Metuchen, N.J.: Scarecrow Press, 1972.

HOULE, C. O. *The Design of Education.* San Francisco: Jossey-Bass, 1972.

HOULE, C. O. *The External Degree.* San Francisco: Jossey-Bass, 1973.

International Congress of University Adult Education (Issue devoted to programs of various countries), May 1972, *11.*

Bibliography

JACOBSON, M. S. *Night and Day: The Interaction Between an Academic Institution and Its Evening College.* Metuchen, N.J.: Scarecrow Press, 1970.

JOHNSON, B. L. *Islands of Innovation Expanding: Changes in the Community College.* Beverly Hills, Calif.: Glencoe Press, 1969.

JOHNSON, E. I. "The University, Adult Education, and Our Society of Cities." *Adult Leadership,* 1966, *14.*

JOHNSTONE, W. C., AND RIVERA, R. J. *Volunteers for Learning.* Chicago: Aldine, 1965.

KATZ, I. "Higher Continuing Education." In A. Knowles (Ed.), *Handbook of College and University Administration— Academic.* New York: McGraw-Hill, 1970.

KERR, C. *The Urban-Grant University.* Paper presented at the Centennial Meeting of the Phi Beta Kappa Chapter of the City College of New York. New York, October 18, 1967.

KERR, C. "New Challenges to the College and University." In K. Gordon (Ed.), *Agenda for the Nation.* Washington, D.C.: Brookings Institution, 1968.

KERR, C. *The Uses of the University.* Cambridge, Mass.: Harvard University Press, 1963.

KERTESZ, S. D. (Ed.) *The Task of Universities in a Changing World.* Notre Dame, Ind.: University of Notre Dame Press, 1971.

KIRKPATRICK, J. *College Control in Michigan.* Yellow Springs, Ohio: Antioch Press, 1929.

KLOTSCHE, J. M. *The Urban University—and the Future of our Cities.* New York: Harper and Row, 1966.

KNOWLES, M. S. *The Adult Education Movement in the United States.* New York: Holt, Rinehart, and Winston, 1962.

KNOWLES, M. S. *Higher Adult Education in the United States.* Washington, D.C.: American Council on Education, 1969.

LINDEMAN, E. C. *The Meaning of Adult Education.* Montreal: Harvest House, 1961.

LIVINGSTONE, R. *On Education.* New York: Macmillan, 1964.

Bibliography

LONDON, H. "University Without Walls: Reform or Rip-Off?" *Saturday Review,* September 16, 1972, *55.*

MC CONNAUGHEY, J. "The Role of the University in the Solution of Urban Social Problems." *Comment* (Wayne State University), 1967, *10.*

MACKAY, A. L. "The University Education of Mature Students." *Universities Quarterly,* March 1968, *22.*

MACLURE, S. "England's Open University." *Change,* March–April 1971, *3.*

MC MAHON, E. E. *The Emerging Evening College.* New York: Teachers College, Columbia University, 1960.

MC NEIL, D. R. "The University and Adult Education." *Adult Education,* 1963, *9*(2).

MAYHEW, L. B. *Graduate and Professional Education, 1980: A Survey of Institutional Plans.* New York: McGraw-Hill, 1970.

MEAD, M., AND BYERS, P. *The Small Conference: An Innovation in Communication.* Paris: Mouton, 1968.

MEDSKER, L. L., AND TILLERY, D. *Breaking the Access Barrier.* New York: McGraw-Hill, 1971.

MOSES, S. *The Learning Force: A More Comprehensive Framework for Educational Policy.* Syracuse, N.Y.: Syracuse University, Publications in Continuing Education, Occasional Paper No. 25, 1971.

NATIONAL COMMISSION ON TECHNOLOGY, AUTOMATION, AND ECONOMIC PROGRESS. *Technology and the American Economy.* Washington, D.C.: Government Printing Office, 1966.

NEWMAN, F., AND OTHERS. *Report on Higher Education.* Washington, D.C.: Government Printing Office, 1971.

NEWMAN, F. "A Preview of the Second Newman Report." *Change,* May 1972, *4.*

ORGANISATION FOR ECONOMIC CO-OPERATION AND DEVELOPMENT. *Equal Educational Opportunity.* Paris: OECD, undated.

OSMAN, J. "The Bias of Urbanization." In *The Emerging City and Higher Adult Education.* Atlanta, Ga.: Southern Regional Education Board, 1963.

Bibliography

PIFER, A. "Is It Time for an External Degree?" *College Board Review,* Winter 1970–71, *78.*

REID, R. H. *American Degree Mills: A Study of Their Operations and of Existing and Potential Ways to Control Them.* Washington, D.C.: American Council on Education, 1959.

ROSENTRETER, F. M. *The Boundaries of the Campus: A History of the University of Wisconsin Extension Division, 1885–1945.* Madison: University of Wisconsin Press, 1957.

SHANNON, T. J., AND SCHOENFELD, C. A. *University Extension (The Library of Education).* New York: Center for Applied Research in Education, 1965.

SLOAN COMMISSION ON CABLE COMMUNICATIONS. *On the Cable: The Television of Abundance.* New York: McGraw-Hill, 1971.

SMITH, G. K. (Ed.) *New Teaching, New Learning.* San Francisco: Jossey-Bass, 1971.

SMITH, R. M., AKER, G. F., AND KIDD, J. R. (Eds.) *Handbook of Adult Education.* New York: Macmillan, 1970.

SOLOMAN, R. J. "Giving Credit Where It's Due." *Educational Record,* Summer 1970, *51.*

SPURR, S. H. *Academic Degree Structures: Innovative Practices.* New York: McGraw-Hill, 1970.

STRINER, H. E. *Continuing Education as a National Capital Investment.* Washington, D.C.: W. E. Upjohn Institute for Employment Research, 1972.

STROTHER, G. B. "Report of the View-of-the Future Committee." *NUEA Spectator,* June 1972, *36.*

TAUBMAN, P., AND WALES, T. *Mental Ability and Higher Educational Attainment in the 20th Century.* Washington, D.C.: National Bureau of Economic Research, 1972.

THOMPSON, F. C. *The New York Times Guide to Continuing Education.* Prepared by the College Entrance Examination Board. New York: Quadrangle Books, 1972.

"Three Hundred Years on the Same Piece of Land." *Life,* September 17, 1971, *71.*

Bibliography

TROUTT, R. *Special Degree Programs for Adults: Exploring Non-Traditional Degree Programs in Higher Education.* Iowa City, Ia.: American College Testing Program, 1971.

UNION FOR EXPERIMENTING COLLEGES AND UNIVERSITIES. *Universities Without Walls: A First Report.* Yellow Springs, Ohio: Antioch College, 1972.

VALLEY, J. R. *Increasing the Options.* Princeton, N.J.: Educational Testing Service, 1972.

VERMILYE, D. W. (Ed.) *The Expanded Campus.* San Francisco: Jossey-Bass, 1972.

WEBER, M. M. "The Post-City Age." *Daedalus,* Fall 1968, 97 (4).

WITHEY, S. B., AND OTHERS *A Degree and What Else?* New York: McGraw-Hill, 1971.

Index

Index

Index

Utah, community use of school facilities in, 17

V

Visiting as enrollment option, 73
Vocational studies, shift to, 37-38

W

WEBER, M. M., 48
Wisconsin, University of: college of continuing education at, 41; service role of, 36-37